MW01675513

An Hour More With Geoff

Vita N. Bernardo

Scripture references are taken from the New International Version, 1978, The Zondervan Corporation, Grand Rapids, Michigan.

Copyright © 2006 Vita N. Bernardo

All rights reserved. No part of this publication may be reproduced, stored in a retrieval system, or transmitted in any form or by any means, electronic, mechanical, photocopying, recording, or otherwise, without the prior written permission of the publisher.

ISBN: 0-9774928-4-2

Published by:
Holy Fire Publishing
531 Constitution Blvd. Martinsburg, WV 25401
www.ChristianPublish.com

Printed in the United States of America and the United Kingdom

For Phoebe

For Moms

For Dad

An Hour More
With Geoff

Chapter
One

Daun bagaikan menari di dahan
Ketika angin berhembus perlahan
Angin, angin, bertiuplah terus
Sejuk nyaman mengelus

Lemah lembut dan makin mengeras
Angin bertiup segar
Lemah lembut dan makin mengeras
Desir daun terdengar

Lying down on the mattress that my mom put on the floor of my ex-room and feeling my pats on her back while I was singing that Indonesian kid's song, my 18-month-old baby, Phoebe, seemed to find comfort to sleep. The room was dark but the light outside was still able to help me see her eyes which were getting drowsier and finally closed. One side of her face lied on the pillow which made her chubby cheek pressed and her opened-tiny mouth curled. She looked more and more adorable with this sleeping position, lying down on her tummy, her favourite position since she was a little bitty baby as I noticed, but I didn't let her do it often until she was seven months old, worrying about the crib death that happened to some babies.

Everybody loves Phoebe. They just fall in love with her at the first sight they see her. She always becomes the central of attention but I'm not sure whether or not she likes it. Her mommy doesn't! With her appearance and radiant face, she is always attracting everybody's eyes and brings joy to them that they cannot resist for not smiling or even touching her. Bringing Phoebe means bringing her new fans! People on the streets, people on the malls, at the hospitals, at the airports, at the banks ... She was even able to make one doctor fall from getting her chair back being too busy to take her pictures through her cell phone and forgot to write the prescription for her sickness! At one of the shopping centers, two cashiers there were busily admiring her that they didn't realize I had been standing there for some minutes to get served!

She was a daddy's girl, her daddy was really proud of her! "She is my little pumpkin, Honey!" my husband, Geoff, said to me one day.

I know. When there were some new babies coming and we had a chance to see them all, he would ask, "Now after you saw those babies, do you still believe that they are cuter than Phoebe?" I must agree with him, just like one of his cousins said that Phoebe is the cutest baby he's ever seen so far. It's not because Phoebe is our child but it's true that she has a unique type of look.

The news about our pregnancy was a great joy to everybody and to some it had even been something they were looking forward to for so long. We found out that we were expecting when we visited Geoff's parents at their cottage in Muskoka late August 2003. I didn't really have problems with my pregnancy, other than craving Indonesian food for several times. However, since there are some Chinese restaurants in Peterborough, that helped me reduce my craving.

There were times when I couldn't hold my appetite of Indonesian food so I went to get some ingredients in any Asian stores available. I even wrote my mom in Jakarta to send me some foods or spices, so I was so happy to get the package coming from her one day but got disappointed to find out that one of my favourite foods was banned by Canadian customs in Vancouver. The reason was unclear other than because it contained meat.

I was always looking forward to the weekends. Usually Saturdays and Sundays after the church, Geoff would ask me to go out with him, to the lakes or just driving around. I loved it and more because we would eat out in a restaurant and he would ask me to choose. Ever since I passed my two-month-pregnancy, I noticed my appetite was getting bigger so was his. We both gained so much weight within a short period of time.

"Do we still have pasta at home, Honey?" he asked me one Sunday morning on our way back home after the first service of the church we attended.

I didn't answer him right away, not because I didn't know the answer but I knew we were not going to a restaurant for lunch while I really wanted Chinese food, not pasta.

"I think we still have some pasta", I answered. I really hoped he would notice my cold reaction to his question and would ask me, as usual even when we were still dating, what kind of food I wanted to eat, but this time, nothing. I was not really moved to tell him how much I wanted Chinese food as we had discussed about saving our money. We needed to reduce the frequency of eating out in the restaurants.

"Great, so we are going home and I'll make lunch, how's that?" I had suspected he would say that.

It took for about fifteen minutes from Peterborough to our house in Cavan. I always loved to be on the roads back and forth enjoying the views of lakes and woods in any season, but not on that Sunday though. I was so hungry, I ate for two but I didn't want pasta or pasta of any kind!

Once we arrived at home, he enthusiastically grabbed everything he needed to make our lunch but I just sat down there on our breakfast table. I saw two blue jays on our bird feeder at the back yard, eating the bird seeds he put two days ago. They were really enjoying their lunch and yet I was sitting at the table not enthusiastic, waiting for our lunch to get ready. It would be pasta.

"Oh, no, there's no meatball left!" he said after opening the freezer but still trying to find it somewhere else. Now what, pasta without meatballs? I hope he was just joking!

He put the plates on our breakfast table, full of pasta covered with the sauce but without meatballs, how would it taste? He took parmesan cheese and shook the container on our plates, I noticed that it was not much left too so we had to share which means only small amount each of us would get even though I knew he would give me more from his portion. Pasta without meatballs and just a little bit of parmesan, truly I lost my appetite, my hunger was gone. He finished his lunch but I didn't touch it at all.

He spent some minutes watching me playing with the fork. We were both just silent, he knew that I wouldn't eat my pasta but he seemed to wait for my words.

"I'll take it later", I broke the silence. Being married for several months, there were some cases where our communications needed some improvements.

He nodded then went to his office room just next to the kitchen. I wrapped my plate and put it into the fridge. I didn't know when I would take it but I started to feel guilty for not being thankful to him for having prepared our lunch. I would cook for our supper and make sure it was going to be enjoyable for both of us. Geoff was not really picky about the food, he would take anything I served for him and would like to try anything that was so new to him, so that pasta without meatballs and only a small amount of parmesan cheese was not a big deal for his appetite, he took it easily.

I thought I was just becoming more sensitive during this pregnancy and wanted my husband to spoil me. But I should confess that he deserved the empathy too. I didn't really get many pregnancy sicknesses, he was the one who went to bathroom several times in the middle of the night and had some headaches!

"I guess, I am taking all of your pregnancy discomforts", he said to me one early morning, at about two o'clock, going back to our bed from bathroom. We were still awake at that time, chatting and discussing about the names for our baby.

I smiled not because I was not feeling sorry for him but I remembered him several times saying that he and his dad were just like camels, could retain the fluid for hours without having any urge to go to bathroom. It certainly helped them in doing outdoor things especially fishing when they had to be on the lake for so many hours and days.

Fishing ... it's one of his family traditions. Both of his grandpas were the avid fishermen, his dad still fishes until today and they spent a lot of time to go fishing to where the fish called them. Geoff was really living in it since he was really young.

"Fishing teaches me how to be patient," he said, something I totally agree with. But fish was not just the only creature he liked. Any kind of birds of which owls were his most favorite ones, lizards, frogs, insects and spiders, those were some of his interests too. He ever got bad wound on his leg trying to catch a frog from a pond when he was still a kid. As to the lizard type, he was amazed to see the chameleon, crocodile, alligator, komodo, gecko even *cicak,* a small lizard that he saw in Indonesia crawling freely on the wall, he enjoyed to see them all. He would proudly show everybody the birthday gift that I gave to him some times back. It was a tarantula spider, a dead one of course, hung on the wall of the hallway of our house in Cavan.

Chapter Two

"I'll go ice-fishing with John tomorrow, Honey, and I'm leaving around 5.30 in the morning, if you don't mind", he said after hanging up the phone.

That was John on the phone, his best man at our wedding. They had been close friends since more than twenty years ago. Geoff knew John thru his fiancée, Leanne, who went to the same church at Hilltop. Geoff shared all of his fishing stories with him who is an avid fisherman as well, so they became close. There was another guy who spent quite number of times fishing together when Geoff was still single and was his groomsman at our wedding, Ron is his name. He lives in the area where we always went by to go to and back from Geoff's parents' cottage. Every time we went by Ron's place, Geoff always asked, "Shall we call Ron, Honey?" or "Shall we stop by at his workshop for a short visit?" It was never a short visit actually, it ended up being a long chat between them two. Both of them just loved to share the stories and experiences. He found Ron to be someone who is so funny and humorous. With his expertise and experiences in taxidermy, there were so many stories to share about Ron which Geoff could tell in details.

I never said no when Geoff wanted to go fishing. He loved it and he needed it. It was his passion. He would go crazy if he didn't get out of the house even within just a day. I used to love staying at home but living with him now even only within some months, had brought another experience to me. I started to like fishing, he taught me many things how to catch fish. If the weather was not promising for fishing then he would arrange the trip to sightsee with his heavy vehicle which he bought in 2001. A blue-4 Wheel Drive-standard-Nissan-Pathfinder which is specially designed for cross-country roads. He touched it up with a nice inside interior with leather seat covers. Great truck. When we went fishing at St. John lake some times ago after our wedding, my oh my, the road was so bumpy, rocky, slippery, muddy that we jumped here and there and made the truck tilting sharply right and left. I could hear the cracks on the roof of his truck, it must be his canoe rubbing the ropes which tied it. I was worried the truck would break and we got stranded in the middle of nowhere yet no signal for the cell phone! But Geoff looked calm busily handling the steering-wheel with confidence. That eased me. It was fun!

“So do you want me to prepare your lunch now for tomorrow?” I offered my help while watching TV, lying down on the couch with my eight-month-old-pregnancy. I didn’t stand up right away, the baby moves I felt in my womb were too good to get missed.

“Ah, don’t worry about that, I’ll make it tomorrow before I go”, he said and went back to his chair watching TV, his favourite game was on ... hockey!

The game was not yet over, they were showing commercials when he stood up and started to pack up the things he needed to bring tomorrow. I did fish several times, even before we met. I did go fishing with friends from work on the ocean in Jakarta and I caught good amount of fish even though they were not big ones. I used the regular rods, the ones with rolling lines, whatever it is called. Geoff did it too but he became more and more interested in fly-fishing and ended up becoming an expert on it. He had gone fly-fishing for so many hours, so many days in a year for so many years in so many places all across Canada. He was not just an avid fisherman but he was too an avid outdoor guy who had traveled to so many amazing places in Canada with his one and only canoe that he bought some years back. Five thousand bucks, he said. He loved his canoe. He loved paddling and spent most of his fishing time with it.

I had a chance to find a videotape about the fishing contest in 1994 he participated. I noticed that it was operated and edited by Karen, his only sister and sibling.

"I don't know what to say about this guy, but his qualifications to win this contest are far exceeded", said the spokesman of the event before continuing his speech and announcing the winner. Geoff came forward to receive the prizes as the winner of most of the categories at the contest. He was even chosen as the 1994 Angler of the Year and he got a Ford truck as one of the prizes. All the trophies he got were put on the top of his fishing cabinet he designed. Most of the fishes he caught were mounted and put on the wall in his fishing room, right beside our bedroom. They are all nice to see, most got the world records. He was so careful about his collection, he even had a special guy who engraved the tag to label each fish. He wouldn't let the blinds on the window open as the sun can fade the fishes.

Besides the cabinet, another thing he liked to tell was his fly-tying table. It's his own design as well, made from the same wood, oak. So nicely and professionally made. One of his friends did it. At a glance, since it has a lid which closes the table, it looks like an organ. It has so many shelves where he put the materials to make the flies. He made hundreds of them and they really look like real flies! I'm amazed. That is why it's called fly-fishing. You use flies on your hook instead of worms, shrimps or minnows.

"Throw the line as hard and far as you can, once it gets to the water, then pull it slowly but constantly. Once you feel the fish grabs your fly, then pull it hard, the fish will be in your hook", he taught me one day while holding my hands to make sure I was holding the rod right. We practiced it one summer afternoon on his lawn, big enough to pretend that we were on the lake. I found it difficult but started to like it.

This ice-fishing, what is it now? He promised to take me ice-fishing someday. Yes, someday and I was really looking forward to it.

Chapter Three

5 o'clock alarm awoke me that morning. Geoff set it up last night as he was leaving at 5.30. He even already got up before the alarm sounded. He forgot to turn it off, I guessed, and I didn't usually get up that early. He got to be doing something in the bathroom, I could tell, as I heard the tap water running. Probably washing his face and brushing teeth. He never took shower to go fishing and that's understandable.

He rushed to turn the alarm off, perhaps he thought that I was still asleep. He went down to the kitchen and within minutes I heard some noise from the frying pan he used to cook the mini sausages for his breakfast. One of his favourite types of breakfast. He liked the omelet to go with it. I could smell the aroma. He was preparing his lunch too but usually it was just light, just apples, two or three pepperonis and a small slice of cheese. I didn't mind to prepare his lunch whenever he went fishing but he didn't want to make me busy for that. One day he brought his lunch that I prepared for him the day before, he said that Scott was jealous to see it.

Scott was his other fishing buddy. They met at the Christian camp one time and just like him with John, they became good friends since Scott loves fishing too. They communicated a lot through phones and emails and always got excited to talk about fishing. Other than bad weather, there was no single season which could block them to go fishing. Even with the temperature far below freezing, that was the best time for them to go ice-fishing.

"The ice should be thick enough to do this ice-fishing, so thick that it could hold even a big truck", Geoff started to explain to me one day. "You do not need a canoe or boat as the lake is frozen, you need a snow mobile to take you to the middle of the lake or any spot you want. Sometimes the ice is so clear that you can see the fishes swimming underneath. You need to have a drill to make a hole on the ice where you put your ice-fishing rod and wait until you got the hit. You have to wear a special jacket to keep you warm and even you need a tent to protect you from the wind. It will be very cold if it's windy, it could even cause frostbites", he continued.

He didn't have a snowmobile or the tent but either John or Scott did, that's why he always went ice-fishing with either one of them or together all. He really wanted to buy a good tent but he hadn't yet found one. He wanted to be sure it was a very good one so it was worth the money spent to buy it.

Here he came, I could hear the friction of the material his jacket made when it rubbed with each other. That jacket was so huge and thick with shocking red and yellow colours. He said that the colours would attract people to help if the ice broke and he fell to the lake. God forbids that would happen to him. Wearing that jacket with his shocking red hat, thick gloves and fishing boots, boom, boom, boom, he looked like Goliath! I can't imagine if I should wear such a costume on the snow, with my petite, well I should say, short posture, people might think I'm a rainbow snowman.

"I'm going now, Honey", he said after giving me kisses on my cheeks and forehead, still lying down on the bed. I always loved to get his kisses. "Be sure to call either Steve or Jenny or Mrs. Stuckey if you need help, okay? I'll turn on my cell phone too but sometimes the signal is so bad to receive the calls on the lake. I'll be back at around seven thirty tonight", he added. "I hope that I could catch some fishes so we could eat them at supper."

Steve and Jenny are our neighbours, a couple who live across the street who are ready to help us anytime, so is Mrs. Stuckey who lives some blocks away from us. Geoff always mentioned their names to me and kept up the relationship with them.

"Or you can call 911 if it's emergency," he continued. "You don't need to pay, it's covered by OHIP and you already got your health card, just show it to them if you can", he said while stroking my head.

"Don't worry, I'll be fine, Honey. Take care and have fun there," I replied, kissing him back.

Within minutes I could hear his car engine started. He had gone. I got back to sleep. I felt cold and I knew the window was open a little, but I was too sleepy and bulky to get up and close it so I let it open. In Springs and Summers, Geoff always opened the window at our bedroom. Just a little bit. He loved to hear the rain so he didn't want to miss it. He always hoped to get the heavy rain and lightning. He also loved to hear the train at nights just few miles away from our house. It gave him the feeling that there was still a life in that remote area. The sound of the frogs, crickets, sometimes owls that came from the woods at our backyard was like a lullaby song to us. And in the day we could hear the birdsong, sound of Canada geese and even turkeys. One morning while I was still sleeping, Geoff woke me up, whispering," I want to show you something, come to the window!" He sounded so excited, enough to double my curiosity to just get up right away to reach the window. There I saw a flock of wild turkeys, probably a dozen, just came out from the woods with their funny sound. "Go grab your camera before they disappear!" I asked him excitedly. It was just a rare experience for both of us to see such a number of wild turkeys on our yard. He managed to take some pictures. Sounds like a zoo, eh? That's the beauty of Cavan. Besides its beautiful hills, lakes, woods and farms surrounding the area, the people and neighbours are wonderful. When I touched its ground for the first time, I felt welcomed. Like home.

The smell of the sausages was still around when I got up and went down to the kitchen. I saw the fatty pan and a plate which Geoff used for his breakfast. He must have forgotten to turn on the fan on the stove when frying those sausages, so I opened the window to get the smell out of the house. I washed the dishes, something I don't mind doing it several times in a day, and prepared my breakfast. I grabbed two slices of whole-wheat bread, took the peanut butter and chocolate bits, sliced the banana and grated the cheese. I put them all together in the bread and toasted it until the chocolate melting. It's so yummy for me but looked yucky for Geoff. He wondered where I got the idea to make such kind of breakfast, it was not inviting at all. Oh, well, it's still healthy though.

After taking one pill of pre-natal vitamin, I got back to my breakfast table, ready to continue folding the papers to make flowers. Ever since I bought a book about origami, I didn't want to do anything else other than trying making new flowers with this origami system.

Geoff had gone just several hours ago but I missed him already. We used to sit together while doing our things, him with his fish paintings for his book and me with my paper flowers. We always listened to our favourite singers and gospel, Bill Gaither and Josh Groban. We love hymns, oldies, classics, but he didn't like high tones of female voice. "They sound like screaming to me," he said. He loved drawing and painting. We have two of his paintings at home, one in the guest bedroom and the other one in the living room. Karen, his sister, was really good at it too. She decorated her bedroom's walls at her house and the walls of the living room at their cottage with stencils painting. So nicely done. "My mom taught me to read and draw since I was two", said Geoff one day. I would say, everybody in their family is an artist.

It was so windy, I could see the trees, branches and leaves swaying fast. There must be so cold on the lake, I assumed. I like the wind but Geoff didn't. "It's not good for fishing if it's windy. The wind will drag my canoe and spook the fish", he said this couple of times.

My baby moved. I put my hand on my tummy to feel it. My baby got to be up from its nappy time. We hadn't yet known about the gender of our baby, we wanted it to be a surprise, but knowing that I loved making paper flowers days and nights, would it be a girl?

While caressing my tummy, my eyes kept looking at the trees outside. The wind blew so hard giving the nice rhythm to the leaves and the branches, swaying here and there. It reminded me of my childhood in Belitung, a small island of Indonesian archipelago where I was born and grew until I was 5. I used to go alone to the bush, enjoying the sunshine and the wind which made the bush dancing. The colour of the soil which was sandy-white made things so clear and bright A perfect spot for me to just play with myself alone. I suddenly remembered the Indonesian kid's song which I used to sing when I was eight, so I sang it for my baby who seemed to move more and more.

Daun bagaikan menari di dahan
Ketika angin berhembus perlahan
Angin, angin, bertiuplah terus
Sejuk nyaman mengelus

Lemah lembut dan makin mengeras
Angin bertiup segar
Lemah lembut dan makin mengeras
Desir daun terdengar

The leaves seem to dance in the branch
When the wind slowly blows
Wind, wind, keep on blowing
Cool and comfort caressing

Tenderly, softly and getting hard
The wind blows so fresh
Tenderly, softly and getting hard
Beats of the leaves are heard

Chapter
Four

Nothing compares to Canada when Fall comes on October. The weather starts to get cool and the colour of the leaves gradually changed to brilliant red, orange or yellow even dark maroon. It is so breathtaking to see everything from the top of the hills. The sunshine will turn the lakes to the mirrors and when it is surrounded with maple trees, then you will want to stay much longer to enjoy it.

Maple trees are everywhere in Canada, that's probably why this country takes it as the symbol of its flag, the maple leaf. Even though they are millions, but you will be so lucky to have maple trees grow around your house where they are ready to give you a scenic view in the Fall. You will have to wait for years to have them grow big, probably they will be at the same age of your kids once they become adults.

Fall 2002 was the second time I landed again in Canada. The first time was in 1998 when I visited Geoff and met with all members of his immediate family. They are wonderful people. Couple of years later, I had a chance to meet with his Uncle and Aunt who spent their vacation in Bali. We had a great time there.

My first visit in Canada was a brief one, ten days only, I spent most of my eligible vacation days from work to visit him. The second time, it was going to be much longer. My manager approved my request to have leave of absence without pay for three months, the reason was we were getting married!

Attending pre-marital course was something really important to both of us especially because we come from two different cultures so we decided to attend one. Since Geoff didn't speak and understand Indonesian, yet he had to know the whole cases given at the course and we were going to live and raise our family in Canada, we then agreed to take it in Canada. His parents had arranged it for us, Pastor Peter from their church who is their close friend, was going to be our tutor.

Fall was Geoff's favourite season. He was always ready with his camera when driving somewhere and I should admit that all the pictures he took turned out to be beautiful ones. Photography was one of his interests besides fishing and drawing, yet I would find later he was so talented in many more.

"I'll take you to Sault Ste. Marie. The colours there are much more beautiful than here. I want you to meet with my friends there too, they are nice people", he said. "We will meet with Greg and Aili, they live in a beautiful country home, you will like it. They are a wonderful couple and I spent a lot of time fishing with Greg", he added.

Sault Ste. Marie was the place where he worked for about one year before he asked me to marry him. He loved the place, he loved his job and his employer wanted him to stay longer but he decided to decline because he didn't feel he got more knowledge and improvement on his skills. He would expect to get much better job especially on his background area, Geographic Information System – GIS. Before taking the job in Sault, the short call for Sault Ste. Marie, he was actually struggling to find one, he said his saving was getting less and less yet the bills were piling up to get paid.

"If nothing comes up soon, I would come to MacDonald to be a burger flipper", he said to me on his email one day. He was serious but he got great news not long after that when the company in Sault decided to employ him even though he had to drive for seven hours for the interview. He didn't have much problem finding an apartment there, but paying two residences through one paycheck is certainly difficult.

Geoff was right, Greg and Aili are really nice couple. They are so friendly, sweet and tender hearted. Entering their house in the Fall will surely make you feel so warm even getting warmer with their hospitality. I noticed there were so many needlework paintings hung on their walls, very nice.

“Aili made them all, aren’t they nice?” Greg gave comments to me when I was admiring each one of them.

“Ah, it’s nothing. I just like doing it”, Aili commented back, shy and low profile.

“There are more, Vita, come here, you see them all? I am even amazed how she made them!,” replied Greg while inviting me to come to the room where I could see many more needlework paintings Aili made, big and small and all are so beautiful.

“Greg!”, Aili said firmly, but I knew she was having nice feelings getting such nice compliments from her husband about her works. She must feel that Greg was too exaggerating but he was not, he just felt so proud of his wife, the feeling I’ve ever got from Geoff as well.

Some weeks back when we invited his parents to have supper together with us, he asked me to cook Indonesian recipes while he made the dessert. He so liked my *risoles* probably just like the egg roll here with chicken, carrots, green peas, milk, inside. That was the first time for me to make it, I got the recipe from my sister's cook in Indonesia and I am not a big cook.

"It tastes great!" Geoff commented while chewing it. "Let's save some for my parents and Karen", he added.

"Ah, they don't look okay, I should make them much better than this, look at the burn I made, it's supposed to be clear light brown, not like that", I replied hoping that he would give any other idea to make other type of food. His mom and Karen are very good cook, what would they think to see my burning *risoles*?

"I don't see it matters, Honey, it still tastes good to me and I don't think they will reject", he said. "It's going to be good food to serve before we have our main menu on the table".

His family's visit went smoothly, they all liked the food we provided. "Vita made this, it's called *risoles*, I really like It. Don't you, Dad?" Geoff said proudly while putting one piece of *risoles* to his dad's plate who wanted another one.

Geoff's comments really touched my heart especially when he did it in front of his parents, my parents-in-law-to-be. I felt so special, more and more confident that he was going to be a very good and devoted husband for me who would be proud of his wife. Since then, he frequently gave ideas of inviting some people to come over to our house for lunch or supper and most of the times he asked me to cook. Our friends from the church especially the international students had come to our house for several times now, either we cooked for them or they brought food for us. Now and then whenever I was cooking at the kitchen he always asked, "Are you making a spectacular food for me, Honey?" while hugging me from my back and giving a warm kiss. He always gave compliments to me whenever I cleaned up the house. "Thank you for making our house neat and tidy," he said and hugged me again and again.

"How do you meet?" Aili's voice woke me up from my daydream. I didn't know whether she asked me or Geoff but any of us could answer this. I looked at Geoff who at the same time looked at me too, he knew then he would answer.

Having no response for a minute while pouring the tea for us at their kitchen table, Aili looked at us both wondering why it took time to answer her question. No, that was not difficult to answer, we were not surprised at it as well because we got some folks who asked the same question before. It was just who between me and Geoff would respond.

"We met on-line", Geoff replied smilingly. I waited to get her and Greg's reaction who seemed to have similar question.

"Really?" asked Aili with eyes opening wider. Greg just said "oh!" and smiled.

Meeting someone on-line for serious relationship, hard to believe that would work. You can't trust your neighbour who lives just a block away from you and now you build a relationship with someone from half of the globe of where you live?

Yeah, a miracle happened to us and it didn't happen in a blink of an eye. It took seven years for us to get to know each other. It started when I was just pretty new to the internet thing and while I was learning it more and more, I stuck on a Christian website where we both met. At the age of thirty three who never had a date with any guy, I was actually making myself ready to live single for the rest of my life but my hope to find a nice single Christian guy was never gone.

We exchanged emails since then, handwritten letters, cards, gifts, pictures, packages, even phone calls and we became so close. We then decided to meet face to face. But they all didn't guarantee everything we had done had made us really know and understand each other. There had been so many frictions between us, back and forth, ups and downs, goodbyes and hellos again. Geoff changed my days, he made me motivated to face a new day because I knew I would get his email, even twice in a day. That was when my days were fine but when he felt something wrong with our relationship, he challenged me a lot until I was tired to answer. At the times when he said we would better break up, I felt so empty. He'd been filling up my days with his presence, his stories, his experiences and now nothing I got. I was so broken hearted.

Reading his profile, I knew he was fond of fishing but the more I talked to him the more I knew how thirsty he was for talking about God. His love to God was so deep and true, he would not mind to get someone felt offended because anything that he said and believed to be true. Almost all subjects we had discussed were all about his spiritual life, church, people and most of all, God. He challenged me a lot on these things and I would admit I failed to make him satisfied with my answers. I took this as the reason why he thought we better break up. I felt hurt but I still have God who cares, so I prayed and prayed and asked Him to tell me if I put Geoff more than Him. I was too missing Geoff though to just totally stop our emails so we agreed to keep communicating and that took years.

"Vita, I want you to open this website sometime today and give your answer before your day is over", Geoff emailed me on June 21, 2002 with this request. I did. It was a nice website he made for me. He put many pictures of me there and he put some of our oldies favourite songs as well as our favourite hymns. Good job, Geoff! I didn't have any idea how long he spent to make this website. I clicked the second page and was shocked to get his question: "Will you marry me?" What's this? I couldn't believe my eyes! But I knew Geoff would not do it as a joke.

So empty in the room, most of the employees were having time to see the world cup on TV downstairs. It was between England and Brazil. So quiet in the room where I was seated. I could hear my heart beating faster after getting Geoff's proposal on-line. I asked my friend, Dawina, to tell me that it was a serious one. She laughed, patted my shoulder and softly screamed, "Ha, congratulations, *Kak*! He is surely serious, see, he provided you with the answering button as well, so he's waiting for your response" she said. She was right, yes, there was another button for me to respond, yes or no.

I got my mom's call from home to ask me go home on time. Her voice sounded surprised but I didn't have any idea what was going on there. Did Geoff call her about this news? I doubted.

Everybody in my family was watching TV when I got home. Everybody was having world cup fever, I believed, so was I, but there was another thing happened that day which I should care more now. The game between US and German, if I was not mistaken, ended with 2-1 for German. The US team was really making a record for being able to go to a quarter final and gave a tough play to German team who has been superior in this football game for decades.

Knowing my arrival, my mom asked me to just go to my room. Everybody followed me and I couldn't believe my eyes when I saw so many colourful rose-bouquets. They were from Geoff! I explained them what had happened and they were so surprised! My mom got silent but I knew through her eyes that it was a happy news for her. Finally her second daughter, me, would get married! My elder sister kneeled down and said, "Thank you, Lord!", and kissed me.

Geoff called me that night and I thanked him for making that day so special to me with his question and so many roses he sent which I believed he ordered on-line. He popped up the same question again over the phone and I certainly said yes.

Being so curious and knowing that our relationship was not a smooth journey, I asked him why he decided to finally ask me to marry him. His voice became serious, he paused for a second.

"Well, I know that we were struggling with our relationship in some cases, some conflicts, disagreements, miscommunications occurred but you stuck on me, you came back to me right away and you tried hard to make our relationship better and you really changed my attitudes. I have given you the time to go away from me and go on finding somebody else that you think you will be more comfortable with, yet you were still there for me. Did it answer your question?" he asked. "But you need to know it again that I don't have decent meals like my parents do and I don't live in a palace, but I am committed and I will do my best to make us both happy. You have all my unconditional love."

That's what I need the most.

Chapter Five

The political situation in Indonesia which was getting worse forced us to change the plan to have the marriage held in Indonesia. It was certainly not a good news for my families especially my siblings and cousins who had been waiting for it for so long. It was too good to get missed, they said, but they respected our decision and gave supports. I knew it was so hard for them to see me gone this time because I was getting married without their presence and would live in Canada for good to start our life as husband and wife, so we didn't know when we were going to meet again.

"Everything has been set up, Vita, the invitation has all been sent out. We are just waiting for the bride to come," said Geoff one day on his email. I was still at work, finishing my job at my last working days in Indonesia. I was getting married on June 14, 2003 in Canada yet I was still in Indonesia on April 2003.

"My resignation has been approved and I got the visa as well so I'm ready to go and be there as planned," I replied to ease him. We were actually concerned about this visa thing, it was so difficult to get a visa for any Indonesian traveling abroad but I didn't find any problems though getting Canadian visa. I took it as the answer of my prayers and indeed Geoff and his church friends at their small group prayed for me as well.

I started to pack my stuff and made the workstation ready for my replacement to continue my job as the executive secretary to the President Director of IBM Indonesia. Thirteen years working there had made this company like a home to me. I became so sentimental in so sudden but I had confirmed myself to get ready leaving this company which had given me so many memories.

I grabbed the picture of me and Geoff by the Christmas tree from my working desk, it was taken when I was with him for pre-marital course. We both looked so happy, our wedding was coming. I looked at my finger; I was wearing his engagement ring now. I got it just few days before Christmas 2002. This recalled me again the moment when I got it.

"Honey, there is one Christmas ornament still left on the dining table, could you please put it on the tree?" said Geoff one morning when he was taking a shower. That was the time when we had completed our pre-marital course and few days left for me to stay in Canada before I went back home to Jakarta.

I came to his dining room and found a small green container on the table. It was heavy and I think too heavy to be put on the Christmas tree. I looked at it thoroughly and realized that it had a lid, so I opened it and smiled to see what was in it. It was the engagement ring and now it's on my finger. This was really a nice thing to remember.

Geoff and his parents had indeed set up everything. I would say, eighty percents of the preparation had been done and they needed my involvement to finish the rest like choosing the flowers, preparing the truffles, wrapping up the gifts for the guests, choosing the wedding cake, making the programs and some more. They had done a tremendous job for our wedding, Geoff even arranged to get Indonesian traditional music called gamelan, performed at our wedding and got an Indonesian pastor, Pastor Polin, to take an important role at the ceremony in the church. He would say his vow in Indonesian, wasn't it amazing? He did these all to make me feel so happy on our special day, I was really touched by what he had done. Not so many guys wanting to get involved in such detailed things even though it's for their wedding.

We picked up my mom and my sister, Oline, at the airport who arrived in Canada to attend our wedding. Having been in the plane for thirty three hours since they took the flight through Europe, worrying about SARS which attacked some Asian countries at that time, they really looked tired but so happy to see us waiting for their arrival. It was the second time for them to see Geoff since the last time he met with my family in 1998. They, especially my mom, just liked him right away and were so happy to know that he was going to be a part of our family.

Geoff was glad to communicate with my mom and Oline as both parties didn't speak each other's language but they managed to understand what they meant with this and that. Geoff always liked to learn foreign languages and he tried his best to practice his Indonesian that he learned from the books, dictionaries, CDs and cassettes. He was struggling though and I couldn't always satisfy him with the answer when it came to why this, why that, so I asked him to just accept as it is. I am not a good teacher, I admit.

"Indonesian language is so easy to learn," I said it to him one day, "as it doesn't recognize tenses such as past, future, present. The verbs do not change, we just need to add another word indicating time if we need to mention the time when something is done."

He disagreed with me that it is easy but I admired his enthusiasm.

Anyway, we were ready for our wedding soon!

Chapter
Six

Geoff finished his wedding vow in Indonesian smoothly, the guests really clapped for him. The vow was long enough to get repeated yet it was in the language which was so foreign to him. I was proud!

The ceremony took an hour; it was done beautifully even though I almost fell during my walk on the isle to get to the altar where Geoff and his two good friends, Ron and John, were waiting and my sister, Oline, as my bridesmaid, at the other side. I didn't want to get so emotional at the ceremony so when I saw my mom standing in tears at her seat, I tried hard to keep my concentration going without any tears.

The reception was done smoothly too, everybody was happy and enjoyed the meals served for them. As the welcoming refreshment, Geoff ordered it from the Indonesian restaurant in Toronto. They liked the gamelan and the teary moment when my mom put the *ulos*, a Batakese traditional shawl, on our shoulders with her blessings and put another to Geoff's parents' shoulders to welcome them to our family.

We arrived at our hotel still wearing our wedding apparels. We felt so tired that we just needed to have a long sleep. We still had a big project that awaited us ... our honeymoon! We were going to drive to three provinces of Canada and I was looking forward to it. I always love long drives, with Geoff for sure. He was a very good driver, I always felt comfortable sitting beside him at his car. But first we needed to take my mom and my sister to the airport as they head off home, that means another thirty three hours for them to get to Jakarta. I was just too happy to cry to see them gone.

Quebec, the first time I touched this land. Very nice province but I'm not sure I could live there. The people speak French and I don't. They don't speak English or they don't want to learn it, whatever, it must be hard for a non-French-speaking people to live there.

"*Bonjour, avez-vous fait votre choix*?" asked the waitress ready to write down our order. It was a cozy restaurant, full of people and no surprise, I didn't hear anyone speaking English. They all spoke French, I would say, Quebec French not France French, even though I don't know the difference between them two. Their breakfast menu looked so yummy, I don't understand most of the words written there but at least the pictures on the menu could describe it.

"*Oui, je veux une omelette et un chocolat chaud, s'il vous plait*", Geoff answered, "*... et ma femme*, what do you want, Honey?" he asked me.

I knew Geoff learned French when he was at school but I didn't know he spoke it that well. I looked at him giving a hint that I wanted the same menu as his even though I would like to have another one, I just didn't want to get bothered with this language thing.

"First time to do once we got to our inn in News Brunswick is to arrange the phone line to be used for me for about an hour to do the interview with MNR guys," he said while eating his omelet. "I should get ready for this interview, not many chances like this offered to the public," he added.

I listened to him and nodded. I know how much he wanted the job in MNR Peterborough as he liked the city, the location and the job for sure. He had sent his resumes to them several times but no luck even a call for an interview, so when he finally got called by them, he took it as a gold opportunity. It's now or never. He was willing to sacrifice his honeymoon time to get this job, so a phone interview had been set up for them to call him at our inn and he did it well.

For most honeymooners, the ideal place to spend their honeymoon is probably staying in a five-star-hotel near Eiffel Tower in Paris, or by the beach in Hawaii or by the mountains in Switzerland. That didn't happen to us. With his canoe on his truck and some fishing rods he brought, we were ready fishing anytime possible and I didn't mind that as I liked fishing and canoeing, too. But that one time fishing with Ralph, the guy from News Brunswick that we knew to be a good fisherman, was a bit too much for me.

We got to the lake at 7 p.m., it was not deep so they just stood up in the lake wearing the wader. They fished for couple of hours still nothing they got. I decided to just stay in the canoe. As Ralph's instruction, we needed to wait longer as the shads, the fishes, would come at around 9 or 10 p.m. What? I didn't want to sit there to get bitten by mosquitoes which started to come more and more. I was already wearing the mosquito jacket and sprayed myself with repellent, it didn't work. Geoff decided to just go back to our inn when suddenly we heard the splash on the water, getting more and more. Even though it was already dark, we still could see their shiny slippery skin right on the surface of the water, leaping here and there.

"I got one!" we heard Ralph's exciting voice. Minutes later he came with a big shad in his grip. "Throw your line there, there are millions!" he gave instruction to Geoff who then did his command. I waited to see what would happen even though I was so frustrated with those mosquitoes.

"I got one, too! Wow, it's so heavy, it must be a monster!" shouted Geoff minutes later. He was struggling to land the fish so Ralph helped him. It must be not easy for them both, they were becoming farther away from me until I saw them no more. Even their voice disappeared.

It was getting darker, silence around, all I could hear was just thousands of mosquitoes which became more and more vicious. The splash of the shads was even gone.

Five minutes I waited, nothing, six minutes, seven minutes ...

"Honey!" I finally shouted, calling Geoff. "Are you okay there?"

No response. I called him again, still the same. The third time, I called with almost tears in my eyes, I started to feel uncomfortable and scared. Seconds then I finally heard Geoff's voice, the echo, but seemed so far away. They finally appeared. I felt relieved but almost cried for getting left alone on that foreign lake in the dark and had no idea what was going on with my newly-wed-husband. He knew I was upset.

He stood up there outside the canoe with a very big shad in his hands. He grabbed his camera and took some pictures of it. "I need it for my book", he said. Yes, writing a fishing book was another on-going project of his which he hoped to be able to have it published in 2004. He had dedicated himself to do it for years, that was one reason why he didn't have much time to look for a job. As he ever said, he was not worried that he didn't get any job at all. He gave full concentration to write his book and was currently looking for a publisher.

"I'm sorry, Honey, it took a lot of energy to land that shad even though Ralph helped me. I didn't mean our honeymoon to be a fishing trip", he apologized to me once we got to our inn.

“That’s okay, I know you didn’t mean it that way”, I replied. We hugged.

Geoff put his shad in a freezer there at the inn. “I’ll take it later once we are back from PEI. I want it to get mounted”, he said.

The trip to Prince Edward Island was another nice one especially when we were on the bridge to cross the ocean. PEI is said to be one of the world nicest islands and I must agree with that. The hills we saw looked like a giant green carpet, it was so breathtaking. The beach looked so fabulous with sandy hills around.

We didn’t do much in PEI other than walking by the beach, climbing the hills, walking in the woods and taking pictures in the land of lupin flowers. So nice to see them all, we had taken so many nice pictures where we posed romantically.

We ate out couple of times in our favourite seafood restaurant there. Their mussels were so delicious, we enjoyed them. We went fishing on one of the lakes there once, not so many actions happened but the darker it was getting the more fishes came. Splash! Splash! Splash! Thousands of gaspereau dancing and we didn't find problems to hook them. One, two, three ... fifty gaspereaus we caught within just an hour! It was exciting!

Chapter Seven

People said there would be big adjustments in the first years of marriage so often conflicts and disagreements occurred even fights. I don't know whether or not I should agree with that, some couples or even most, they do agree but that didn't happen to our marriage. For sure there had been some conflicts happened between us but Geoff was so patient, caring and understanding that he could melt the situation that tended to get harder for us. He was a much better person compared to when we were still dating. I so enjoyed living with him and happy to be his wife. He'd been so helpful in many ways including getting my application of Permanent Resident approved. I couldn't do many things without him.

He knew sometimes I still felt foreign to this country so he frequently introduced me to his friends, the neighbours and people at the church especially the international students who most of them come from Asian countries. He took the initiative to get to know them or any other new people by greeting them warmly, coming to them or starting a chat.

"Don't wait until somebody comes to you, Honey, we need to be proactive to start knowing somebody especially when they are new comers. Even though it's only you saying hi to them, they will feel welcomed. Get to know as many people you can get, you will never know, they will be used by God to help you someday", he continued.

He had so many friends as a result of his fishing activities and jobs which moved from place to place. He liked them all and had some interesting stories about them that he always liked to share. As much as he liked to befriend with them, still he could not hide his personal feelings about some of their attitudes.

"I don't understand this, they asked me to keep in touch and I did send them emails even gave phone calls yet I never got their replies at all. Oh, people!" he complained with his tender voice. He never raised his voice even when he was upset.

I saw his frustration on that and he was right. So if you need a real true friend who wanted to listen to your problems, he was the one.

As he loved to share stories about his friends, he loved to hear stories about my friends in Indonesia too. He asked me one day whether or not most of my friends are

Christians, I said no, even those who say they are Christian practically they are not.

"If you love your friends, you need to tell them about Jesus," he said firmly. "Tell them about the salvation, about Jesus' love that He sacrificed Himself to free us from our sins and eternal death." I got stunned and felt encouraged to be able to do it right away.

I am happy he was my husband, I had a happy marriage even though it was just new. I wanted to share it with my families and friends in Jakarta so I decided to make a website about my life with him. He supported me. He gave me some references and new books about how to create your own personal website. Since he owned an office at home, he let me use his scanner for the pictures I wanted to put on my web, his computer, his camera, his phone line for the internet ... Oh, he had an angel's heart!

"Any news about your article that you planned to put in a magazine, Honey?" he asked me one day. He asked me again about that article I made about how we met until we got engaged.

"It is finished and I have contacted the magazine in Jakarta, but so far no reply from them", I answered. "It's still in your laptop but I have copied it to a disk."

"Don't you want to have it published? I'll be sad if you don't do it," he replied. I got silent but I would remember what he said. He really encouraged me to write and keep writing. "If you become a writer, you can work from home, Honey", he added. He was right. He knew how much I wanted to work from home if I have to work someday.

"I got an email from the publisher Edwards gave to me. I don't understand, he seems excited to publish my book and sent the agreement to me right away to get signed but I have some questions to him before I sign it as I realize the money I will get is not as much as the work and time I have spent to write that book but he got back to me saying that I better look for another publisher. He must find something on my email which offended him but he didn't mention any. Oh, well, at least he helped me with the list of publishers who might be interested in my book," he said while taking a plate from the cupboard in the kitchen ready for a bowl of cereal. Not just for breakfast, the cereal had been a kind of snack to him whenever he was hungry.

"If I am going to do it independently that means big bucks. I have to pay for the printing, do the ads, hold a conference to promote my book ... we don't have money for that", he continued, his voice became weak. "But if the sales is successful, all money will go to us", his voice changed again, this time sounded enthusiastic.

"I haven't yet heard any news about any of my job applications that I sent. Probably they are still working on the budget for the positions I applied for. But this time around is usually the time when they need people. I have never been struggling like this in the past wanting a job, they always wanted me," he said plainly.

I looked at his face, he didn't look as sad as when he got the news that MNR offered the job to somebody else, this time no sadness nor disappointments, I was glad. But I knew he was having a big burden now on his shoulders to get a job soon. Our money went so fast yet nothing came, we needed money soon to pay our bills. With our child coming soon, his responsibility became bigger. I felt so empathy.

"Honey, probably you are over qualified for any position you applied for or they want much younger people or fresh graduates whom they can pay cheaper," I responded, trying to make him feel better.

"Well, probably you're right, but I don't mind to compete with younger and more skilled guys. I know my capability and I'm always ready for that. I will go wherever the job wants me," he said firmly.

I wished I could help. If there were somebody who was interested in purchasing my paper flowers, I didn't mind to sit days and nights to make more for the money we needed. Geoff didn't think there would be companies who wanted a pregnant woman who would give birth within two month-time. He actually asked me to just look after the house and our child. "Money is my responsibility", he said.

"I will try to call the magazines again in case they need articles for their next edition. They said they would call me back but they didn't. Oh, what happened with these people nowadays?" he expressed his frustration without raising his voice.

Writing was another talent Geoff had. He was a freelance writer of some outdoor magazines in the past. He wrote hundreds of articles most about fishing and he still kept them all in his fishing cabinet. Even though English is not my mother tongue, by reading his emails, I knew his writing skill was far above average. This was probably the reason why he kept encouraging me to write. I do like writing. I wrote some articles for company's magazine years back and that amazed many people that I could bring up a heavy topic for such a big company: how to retain your employees. I met and interviewed some important people of human resources department from several big companies to get their input for this article and it was really a well done job.

"I'll be at my office, Honey, I will continue my mapping and looking for more jobs," he said, walking to his office which was located just next to the kitchen.

He loved the computer, he could sit there for hours learning new applications, programs or browsing the internet. He started a new project recently, mapping. He loved doing it, maps, coordinates, contours of the land, tracks, everything which you learn on GIS, all is new to me. He didn't have problems sitting for days and nights to input the data to make one map and the result was so satisfactory. He always shared with me everything he had done with it even though I do not know anything about it, I listened and tried to understand. Every time one map was about to get finished, he always called me to see it. They looked so nice. He planned to sell them to any institution which needs maps such as outdoor retailers, parks, natural preservation, tourisms even bookstores. He was so sure it was going to be successful.

Again, I loved his enthusiasm.

Chapter Eight

Geoff was watching his favourite TV channel, Sports, when the telephone rang. I asked him to answer. I couldn't pick it up as my hands were wet and soapy washing the dishes. We didn't have a dishwasher, we still didn't see it as an urgent need yet and Geoff still found that washing dishes manually was still faster and cleaner. I didn't mind, I like washing dishes anyway.

I didn't remember what game he was watching, the cheers of the people on TV were so loud, the team had to be doing something which made the audience nervous. At this time like this, Geoff would be so unmotivated to get up from his chair and leave. He was an avid sport fan, any kind of sport he would watch. I don't mind watching hockey and basketball. Ice and figure skating are my favourites, but American football, baseball, even though Geoff so many times explained to me the rules of the game, still I couldn't get them.

I didn't see him coming yet, so I dried my hands with the paper towel to get the handset. We should rush to pick the phone up otherwise it would go to the answering machine after two rings. Geoff ever tried to change it but failed and he couldn't figure it out why and how. Before I had a chance to grab the phone, he suddenly appeared and got it. "Oh, I hope it's not telemarketing guy", I whispered. Imagine if it were one, he would be so upset then.

"Hi!" he greeted. From the tone of his voice, I knew it had to be either his mom or dad. They regularly called each other and shared everything they had done so everybody was updated. This is another good way to still get connected and it's so important to practice it in the family. But one day he told me that after we got married, his family didn't call him as often as before. "Probably they see that we have our own family now, they don't want to interrupt our private life", he was trying to find the answer.

His voice suddenly went weak and he sounded like having a lump in his throat. I stopped my washing, getting more curious to figure out what was going on. It must be sad news. Was it his mom? I knew she has not been really healthy for so long but she always looked fine to me. While drying the plates with the kitchen towel, I stood up by the sink and waited.

He hung up the phone slowly, got up from the chair and hugged me so tightly. He cried! I never saw him crying, only in tears and that was when he was watching somebody on TV talking fondly about Jesus and now right at that time on my shoulders, he was crying!

"What's wrong, Honey?" I asked. No response, his cry became harder. "Hey, what's wrong?" I repeated, holding his face.

"That was my dad telling me that ...," he sobbed, "My sister ... got liver cancer!" he cried out.

"What?" I softly screamed. I hugged and let him cry more and more. It was a very devastating news for us. I couldn't believe it! Karen got cancer? How come? She's been so healthy, so selective with her intakes, so attentive to her health, so clean, so fun, got cancer? What caused that?

For so long I always believed that cancer was not curable so when my dad was diagnosed with lung cancer, I then knew he wouldn't have the chance to live longer since then and I was right. Within just a year after the surgery, he died. Now I need to change my opinion about it that in certain cases, cancer is curable and if you live in the country like Canada, you are lucky as the medical treatment there is a lot, but once it attacks your important organs, your chance to live for as many years as you want is slim. However, miracle happens and hope abides. You will still live without food, without drink, without clothing, but without hope, you will die.

I don't know Karen as much as I know Geoff. We didn't everyday meet as we lived two-hour-drive apart and we didn't exchange calls as often as we did to their parents. All I know is that she was a tender-hearted girl, good communicator, humorous, attentive, sensitive with the things going on among us in the family, full of knowledge, smart, diligent, observant, artistic, very good cook but not as open as her brother in terms of telling who she is to the new people. She once gave away a doll that she bought at the craft exhibition to me as a Christmas gift, an Inuit doll that she loved very much and she said she would never find the same type again in any store or event. She was generous.

I knew her more when she drove me to the malls to find a dress for my mom, or when she took me to see the craft exhibition in Toronto or when she took me to try the hairdresser for my wedding. We had a chance to have lunch together and she told me some of her personal stories which made her decide to live single. She was so attentive to my pregnancy by giving me many pre-natal books and references, a long pillow to give me comforts when I was sleeping with my big tummy and the idea to do the umbilical cord program. She several times called me for not getting worried much about any defect which might happen to our baby. She knew I was troubled with that.

After we got that news, our days were becoming gloomy. Geoff prayed and read the Bible a lot more, searched and browsed the internet many times to get the info about this liver cancer which later we were informed that it was not liver cancer but cancer in her liver. I don't remember the name of it, too complicated to get memorized.

Geoff loved his sister so much, they had been so close since they were little when they did many activities together. The news about Karen really broke his heart, but Karen seemed ready with that. "Only the Lord knows when I was born and for how long I should live", she said after she got the news from her doctor. We knew it was not a good news.

And it's true.

Chapter Nine

Monday, April 19, 2004, Geoff took me to see my gynecologist in Peterborough Medical Center. During my pregnancy, while he was doing his job at home, he was always with me to visit the doctor so he would know what had happened and that really helped me in case I forgot to ask something or I didn't understand the English medical terms. English is not my mother tongue, even though I could speak and understand it well, often I missed out something.

"Your baby doesn't move down yet and it's already thirty nine weeks. I don't want to get any risk to wait any longer, you will need to go through C-Section. Let's schedule it now, on Wednesday, okay?" the doctor said after looking at his digital calendar.

I got silent so did Geoff. I knew such a news would come to us soon because I didn't yet get any symptoms that our baby was ready to get born, but when the doctor finally said it, still made me shock a bit. That was Monday and we would already have our baby on Wednesday, April

21, 2004. One of my nephew's birthday is April 20, my dads' is April 22, Karens' is April 24, my elder sisters' is May 3, Geoffs' is May 5 and the birthday of another sister of mine is May 13, wow, there would be a chance when I send out many birthday cards within a day! Geoff always reminded me to send birthday cards to those who celebrate it in our families. "Do you know why we celebrate the birthday, Honey? It comes from the Bible, we are thankful that God creates and puts us in this world," he said to me one day.

We got everything ready to go to the hospital. We should be there early in the morning at 6 o'clock for the preparation of the surgery which was scheduled at 8 o'clock. Geoff set up the alarm, 5 o'clock, but I was sure we would already get up earlier than that. I was right, we actually couldn't sleep at all!

I was not allowed to take any food, but drinks were okay. Geoff videotaped and interviewed me about my feelings just few minutes before we headed off to the hospital. I knew he got so excited, too. I didn't want to look messy to welcome our baby so I put the lipstick on, thicker than usual.

On our way to the hospital, we were both silent. We were so excited, that was for sure, but I was going to miss my big tummy and the moves that I always enjoyed inside. Soon we were going to hold our baby! I didn't know what

Geoff was thinking but I was sure we were guessing the gender of this baby. I knew Geoff wanted a girl because he said he knew I wanted a girl. He probably noticed the excitement showed on my face whenever I told him all about my nieces. But that was not really true, though. Since we planned to have two kids, I was thinking to have a boy first then a girl, just like him and Karen. Big brother usually takes really good care of his little sister.

"Well, that might be an ideal choice, Honey, but you can see in my family and our friends, girl comes first then boy, my mom and my uncle, Brian, Aunt Marianne and my dad, John and Leanne's kids; MacKenzie and Garrett or Steve and Jenny's kids; Jasmine and Logan, so probably it's going to be a girl and our second child will be a boy", Geoff said smilingly.

Hmmm, this gender thing could be genetic it seems. My dad had two sisters and five brothers, my mom has three sisters and three brothers and I have four sisters and one brother. Fifty percents of the people we talked to said it was going to be a boy and the other fifty said it would be a girl, so? Ah, I wouldn't guess.

"Oh, I forgot to bring the cheque book with me!" Geoff's voice surprised me, tapping his thigh still driving on HWY 115. "I have prepared it last night, I put it by the mirror in the hallway there. Oh, well, I should take you to the hospital first then I'll come back home to take it, is that alright with you?" he asked for my agreement.

Being a new comer in Canada, I hadn't yet got my health card approved. I have been a permanent resident here already starting March 2004 but I had to wait for another month or so to get my health card ready for me to use so that means all medical expenses incurred before that should be on our personal account. Geoff, with his parents' assistance, would pay. Since I was going to get C-section and would stay at the hospital longer than normal birth, the expense was going to be higher. Geoff and his family had been so generous and kind to me, I personally thank them for everything they gave to get me unworried and settled in this country.

"Hi, it's me! Sorry to keep you in tense but I need to tell you guys that Vita has given birth. Guess ... No, it's a girl!" cheered Geoff on the phone when I was already moved to the patient's room. He was talking to his family.

"She was born at 08:25, weighed 8.05 pounds and is 20.5 inches tall. She is really pretty, cute and healthy, Vita is fine too, she was just moved to the room, she is resting now. The name of our baby is Phoebe Kencana, Phoebe means bright and Kencana means gold so she is a bright gold," Geoff continued cheerfully.

I was feeling so sleepy after the surgery but I had to be awake anytime for my baby if she was ready to get fed. I nursed her but since it's my first time, I certainly needed help which I could get from the nurses there. I didn't let her be put in the nursery room even though it was good for the mothers if they want to take a rest but I didn't mind that. It was so joyful to see my baby sleeping on the same bed with me.

I really wanted my parents in law and Karen to come to visit me at the hospital but I understood that they should be home for Karen. To get my mom coming from Indonesia right away was not possible and I didn't know when she was going to see her sixth grandchild even though she ever told me at the airport before she flew back to Indonesia after our wedding that she would come to Canada again if I have a baby. Pastor Rick from our church at Ferndale and some church fellows came to visit me at the hospital. They were all happy for our happiness.

Remembering my mom made me wonder how Geoff handled the conversation with her or any other member of my family in Jakarta to tell the news over the phone since they don't speak English and Geoff didn't speak Indonesian, so we prepared a sheet for this telephone conversation in Indonesian and Geoff had practiced it several times. I hoped he was doing okay with it. It would sound fun but I believed he would do it really well. He did.

Ever since we brought our baby home, Geoff looked differently. He became more protective, more responsible, more attentive, more patient type of guy. He was so proud showing Phoebe to everybody, his eyes shone radiantly and his face expressed the happiest time of his life. Even though Phoebe was still too small to play with her daddy, she was the only reason for him to want to go home fast. He helped me a lot looking after her especially at the first month of our arrival back from the hospital as I was not totally recovered from the surgery.

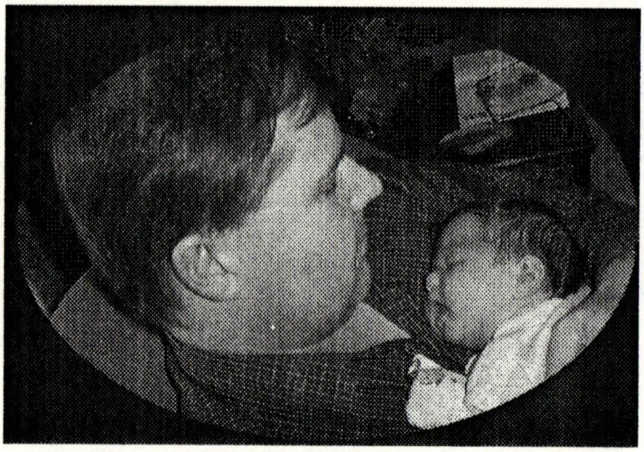

Even though he was getting busier now with his new position as a father, he was not too busy to still remember a special day for me on Mother's Day on May where I got a dozen stems of very pretty big deep red roses and a lovely card in which he thanked me for carrying our child for nine months plus.

As Phoebe grew older, she started to enjoy her daddy's presence who always got excited to play with her. Geoff put so much attention to her growth and got concerned if he thought I fed her too much that she threw up or looked drowsy. He kept taking Phoebe's pictures and videotaping her any moment. He kept reminding me to take her out in her stroller if the weather was nice, it was then he realized that having a baby took his neighbors' attention that he had a family now. He was no more a single guy living in that Fallingbrook corner-lot alone who was many times away from home.

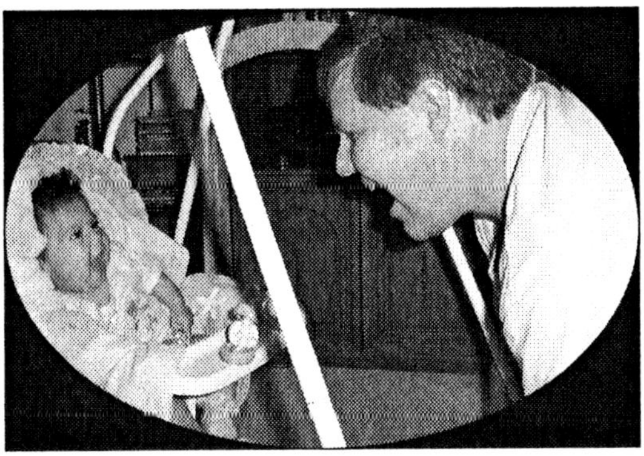

Geoff had been always so attentive to any special day. He cooked and made special meals for my birthday and invited his parents and his sister to come for the celebration and yet I missed his birthday one time! Being so busy with a newborn baby is not an excuse to forget his birthday. I couldn't forgive myself for doing that! But he could!

Chapter Ten

I was nursing Phoebe in her room when I heard a ring. Geoff answered it but I couldn't hear whom he was talking to and what it was about. I really hoped it was a job interview which he waited for. Every time the phone rang, Geoff several times said," job, job, job, come on job", hoping it was a call from any of the companies he put his resume in. I was going to go back to sleep when he came in. He stroke Phoebe who was still with me and kissed her many times.

"That was from Pembroke, Honey, they want me", he said calmly.

I didn't want to right away express my happiness to hear that other than, "Really? Congratulations!" because I knew he had something else in his mind to say.

"It's a 8-month-job contract. The pay is so so but we cannot save much knowing that we have to pay rent and the gas will be costly too to go back and forth," he said. "Unless you want to stay here with Phoebe and I come to visit you every weekend, that will save much", he continued. "But none of us will want that," he added. Of course, I can't imagine staying apart from him for eight months with a little baby!

The job started on June, there was a 3-week-period for Geoff to look for rents and get the vehicle to transport some of our stuffs from home to there. Those were hard jobs which needed high money as well but Geoff did it without any complaint. That's one of his many good characters that I liked a lot. He was a responsible guy, he walked the talks. He managed to find a house owned by an older lady who rented her fully furnished basement, but unfortunately, when we were about to start our day there, she got heart attack which made her have to stay at the hospital for a certain period of time to get ready for the surgery in Ottawa. Without anybody else living at her house, it was so quiet most of the times. It was really a nice place to live in, very nice finished basement, took only five minutes for Geoff to get to work, but not much I could do outside because it's in the country which needs a vehicle to take me to town, yet I didn't have my license.

One day while Geoff was still at work, I wanted to buy some snacks at the convenient store at the end of the road, so I took Phoebe with me by holding her with the sling and covered her really well from the sun because it was so bright and hot. Along the road while I was walking, well, it was not as close as I thought before, several cars stopped and offered me to get in but I declined and told them that I was just going to the convenient store nearby. On my way back to our apartment, a couple who were watering their plants asked me if I needed some drinks or else, I told them soon I would get to where I lived and thanked them for their hospitality. I shared this experience with Geoff and wondered why so many people looked so concerned to see me walking there. "They might think I'm a begging lady", I assumed. Geoff smiled and said, "Sure they did".

Pembroke is a small town which number of population, if it's still the same when we were still there, is 14,000. It takes for about four hours to drive to and from Cavan but that didn't bother him as he loved driving to enjoy the view especially, you can guess, on the Fall. Geoff just loved it especially because it has so many good fishing spots which then led him to join in a fly-fishing club there. It is a small town (by the way, Geoff didn't like a city life at all) with friendly people (well, I would say small towns always have much friendlier people than cities) and a great church, First Evangelical Missionary Church, where we came to worship on Sundays. Most of our friends are from that church with Pastor Alan as the pastor. We loved our Sundays with them just as we loved our church back home in Ferndale Peterborough and we tried to actively participate in their programs.

Geoff so loved to meet with new people, he loved to talk and shared every single thing which he thought would be a good story to share with them. He was a good communicator, too, sometimes when he was telling us about a funny story or an experience, he laughed and laughed until he got tears in his eyes. Often, he already laughed before he was finished.

We just lived for a month in that lady's basement since she wanted us to leave due to her sickness after the surgery. She didn't want somebody else living in her house in such a weak condition and with a little baby with us, it was not going to be good for us too so we had to look for another place to live. We were actually already fed up living in somebody's house no matter how nice and clean it is, we were so missing our private time together as a family without getting worried about this and that and got tied up with their home rules.

Geoff was so busy with his work but he managed to find an apartment in downtown Pembroke but we had to wait until the room was ready for us to use. For the time being me and Phoebe were staying back in Cavan and Geoff again stayed in a room rented by another lady whom he found to be a nice one. This time he was so comfortable to stay there, for a week only, prior to moving to the apartment.

It was already dark when we got to our new apartment. We could say the room was made ready for us in a rush, the furniture was scattered all over the living room and everything was all dusty especially the floors and the blinds. We sneezed many times due to the dust but we were too tired to do the cleaning right away so we just went to bed that night. I couldn't sleep really well though, getting impatient to get tomorrow as I really wanted to clean up and put every single thing in a much better way. I am not a fussy person about the cleanliness and tidiness but the condition of our room there was just too much for me to leave it that way especially with a little baby. I wouldn't expect so much from Geoff that he would be able to help me since he was so busy at work. I didn't mind.

Our life went on nicely in Pembroke, we got more and more new people to talk to especially the tenants in that apartment. Most of them were older people and they really loved to see our little daughter, Phoebe. Even though we could walk to get to the stores for some things we needed to buy, I was not comfortable enough to bring Phoebe in her stroller alone. The traffic was still too busy for me to do that, I didn't want to put our life on risks.

Geoff loved his job and his team at work, he always shared everything happened there with me and was so hopeful that the possibility to get him work there permanently was widely open. Unless he went with his team having lunch outside which was scheduled on Fridays, he always went home for lunch and this really made me glad so I tried my best to cook some varieties of food for our lunch and supper and he loved them all.

"I am so blessed to have you as my wife, you give me a beautiful daughter and you look after us so well. You clean up the house, do the washing and cook many kinds of delicious foods," he thanked me one night. It was one of many compliments I got from him which of course made me flattered.

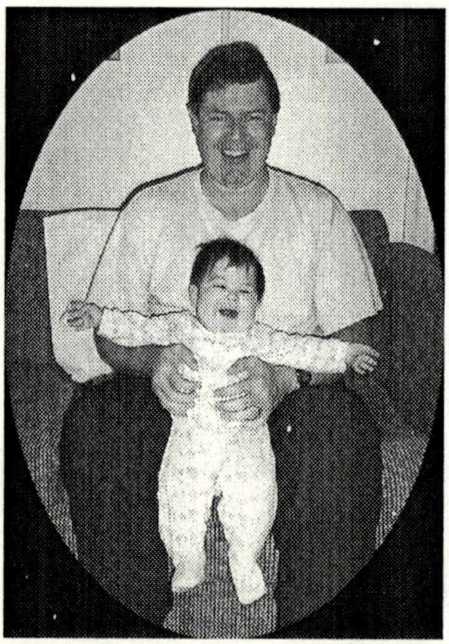

Even though he loved working, he never wanted to be a very busy worker who spent many hours at work. "I want to be with my family as much as I could especially with

Phoebe," he said one day. Every time he got home from somewhere, whenever he didn't see Phoebe right away, he would call, "Phoebe, it's Daddy! Where are you? Where is Daddy's little Pumpkin? There you are!" then grabbed Phoebe into his arms and hugged her tight. He always spared his time to call me from work and whenever he was doing it, he often asked how Phoebe was doing and asked me to put the phone on her ear so he could talk to her. Phoebe recognized her daddy's voice well but her face looked confused and wondered why it came from a thing without a face. Several times Geoff told me how lucky I was to be able to play with Phoebe everyday so he really used his off-work-time to stay with us. He always missed Phoebe, he missed me too, he called us his two "honies". But as much as he wanted to spend maximum days with me and Phoebe, he had to finish his fishing book before he would get too busy to do that.

"I still need one more species to catch for my book before the season is over then I'm done", he said to me one night. He hadn't yet got a potential publisher for his book, most of them said that fly-fishing was not their market so they couldn't sell it. "I will concentrate on my book once my contract here ends and no permanent job for me there", he told me.

I found a new hobby in Pembroke, that was making cards using iris folding system. I did it mostly after I was finished with the house things and Phoebe was sleeping. I just loved doing it. I managed to make many cards and improve my skills even to finally found the way how to create the pattern. I had sent out several of them to my families and friends and they all loved them so I was thinking to sell them and make money.

"My stomach is really hurt and bloated," said Geoff one afternoon from work, bending his back forward and holding the arm of the couch when I was just putting Phoebe on bed. His face looked like holding the pain and I became worried.

"What did you eat at the office, Honey?" I asked him while touching his hand and forehead. His temperature was not high. He didn't go home for lunch that day, he said he had a general meeting where all employees were attending and they provided lunch.

"I don't know whether the food I took is the cause, probably. I ate pizza and salad, probably either one was not fresh anymore," he answered still in the same position.

As far as I remembered, this was the second time he got such kind of illness. The first time was when we were finished with our lunch in one of the restaurants in Peterborough, he believed it was due to the mussels he took there. He was craving them hoping that they were as good as the ones we got in PEI but they made him ill instead. He got bloated for three days, couldn't eat at all.

He lost five pounds as the result. Even though it made him so ill, he didn't want to go to the doctor. "I'll be fine, Honey, nothing to worry about", he said and I was not surprised he would say that.

Now he got the same symptoms again. I asked him to see the doctor but he didn't want to. He said he would feel better if he took hot water shower. He did, he felt better but it took only a minute he felt cold again. His condition was getting worse, he started to feel really cold and he was so shaking. I became panic and started to cry when he kept saying how cold it was yet I already put layers and layers of blanket and bed sheets on him. His temperature was getting high, I measured it using the thermometer his mom gave to us on Phoebe's dedication day, it was 103.2 degrees. It was serious! I wanted to call 911 but he asked me not to, he asked me to just still lay on the bed with him and he prayed. He didn't ask God to heal him but to give me peace and comfort that everything would be alright. He delivered everything in God's hands as He knew His plan is the best. I was so shaky and terrified. My husband was really ill and yet I didn't know anything much about Pembroke as we were just so new to the area. Even though I do believe God really cares, I was so scared that He would take my husband's life. This thought haunted me because just few days before it happened, Geoff made a draft to renew his will and asked me if I would be available to be his executor, the one who is doing things stated on the will from start to finish. "Or it would be too hard for you?" he asked me. I think he didn't need any answer to that, of course. I was not ready at all to live without him and yet our child was still a baby. "Well, leave it that way first, we are going to discuss about it later, it's still a draft anyway", he said while shutting down his laptop.

Amazingly, he felt okay after he said that prayer but I was still panic. He said he didn't understand why he got such a sickness in so sudden, he was sure it was not due to the food he took and he felt strange too. "It must have a connection with my sister", he stated which made me stunned. I know both Geoff and Karen were so close but I didn't know they were that close that Geoff felt what Karen was feeling.

He let me call Pastor Alan if I felt a need to share this burden with him for comforts. I did call him. The time was already 2.30 in the morning, he must be already on bed but apparently he got the call within just two rings. I told him everything and he was surprised to get it because actually he was still up and had a feeling that somebody might call him. "So that person is you, Vita, how is Geoff now? Do you need me to come to your place?" he asked. I told him that Geoff was feeling better so no need for him to come. We just prayed over the phone, I felt relieved afterwards.

Geoff was getting much better the next day, he even went to work without having difficulties, but this time I forced him to see the doctor after work. He did. His blood was taken to get checked, five tubes in total, yet the doctor couldn't find what made Geoff ill that night. Everything was okay and he didn't need to take any medicine at all. That was strange.

Chapter Twelve

Christmas 2004, Geoff took some days off to celebrate it at home. We came to our church, Ferndale Bible church in Peterborough for Christmas Eve. The seats were not full, some people were away to celebrate it with their relatives somewhere else but we got some new folks coming there. Both me and Geoff exchanged the gifts on Christmas morning, it was so fun. I got many gifts from him, from small to big ones. Having Geoff as my husband and father of our child had been God's great gift to me. He was so loving, caring, understanding and patient and now he gave me more.

Last year, we invited some international students to be with us at Christmas day before we went to visit his parents and sister in their residence in Mississauga. Geoff always felt sympathy to those who are far away from their family at this special day so he always wanted to share the joy of Christmas with them by inviting them to come to our house and have brunch together, but since we stayed in two places at that time which were so far apart, it was not possible for us to do that again.

Karen looked so fine for someone who was having a cancer which attacks one of the important organs. She looked so fresh, so humorous as usual and talked a lot. Geoff's mom and dad looked the same way, no sadness on their face. Everybody looked so happy. Geoff and his dad took pictures especially of Karen and Phoebe.

Phoebe was so special to Karen, she loved her so much. I remembered when they visited us at our place in Cavan, Phoebe was still four months old at that time. When Karen held her, Phoebe talked and talked to her a lot while touching Karen's cheeks. I had never seen her talking that much before even to me, her mommy, who spent a lot of time with her. There must be something happening between them two, we don't know what.

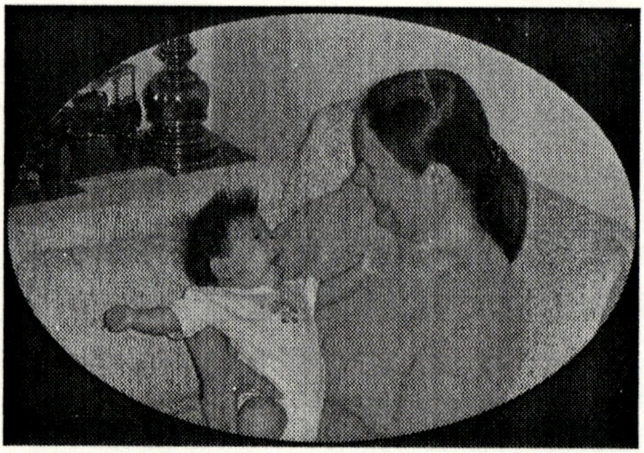

As usual, we got so many gifts from them, all were nice ones. Geoff one day said to me that it was going to be harder and harder to think of what kind of gift should be given to his parents. "They don't seem to need anything now, their house is already packed with many stuffs so let's give something else, something that we could do to help them like cleaning up their house, their garden or their cottage so they don't need to pay somebody to do those kinds of things." he said. A great idea.

Geoff gave a very nice necklace with a jewel pendant to Karen and she loved them a lot. I was surprised though because his plan was to give a locket with his and Karen's picture inside. He seemed to change his mind then. Geoff looked so happy that Karen loved it and I was so happy too. All of them got the album of Phoebe's pictures from us, they loved to receive it.

Karen and their mom were preparing our Christmas dinner when Geoff went to the Christmas tree and seemed to look for something there. They usually put all gifts by the Christmas tree and if it's small enough to get hung in the tree they would do that. His dad who was standing next to him patted his back and asked whether he was looking for something.

"Yeah, I see one gift which is still here, I'll take it", he said. I was still sitting there with Phoebe on my lap. I didn't have any idea what Geoff was doing when he said,"

Oh, it's for you, Honey!" while handing a small wrapped box to me.

I thought he was joking but when I saw my name on the small card on the gift, I took and opened it. Geoff was still standing there and giving me a soft laugh when he saw the change of my face. It was a locket! It gave me a beautiful feeling when I saw both of Phoebe's and his picture in it side by side. Geoff really gave me a big Christmas surprise! So he changed his mind to give such a gift to Karen, he gave it to me instead. He might think that I was the right person to receive it because originally it was my idea for him to give it to Karen yet he changed it in the way of giving me a surprise. He did it!

Christmas had always been a very special day for Geoff but he was troubled by some people's attitude for just ignoring the true meaning of Christmas. On November 2004 at our apartment in Pembroke, he spent some hours to write an article that he planned to put in a Christian journal or magazine. I am not sure whether it will or it will not appear at all on any of them, which magazine and when, I don't have any idea. He didn't tell me further about it. Probably he was too busy with other things or had any other priorities to accomplish or even forgot. One thing I am sure that this article was still in his laptop, unpublished. Well, I am one hundred percents sure he won't mind to let me share it with you. Here is what he wrote:

What Do You Need This Christmas?

Understanding the Facts About God's Entrance into History as a Human Being

Every year a month or two before Christmas I usually get an expected and familiar question asked to me, "What do you need for Christmas this year?" In my small family we have come to expect and make light of this question almost in the same way as my Dad's annual birthday questions – "So, what was the biggest highlight of this past year?" It's almost groanable except for the fact that you know the person asking the question truly does love you and has your best interests at heart. But I am willing to bet that our family is not alone at all in asking this question.

Certainly the advertisers make sure it's asked weeks in advance of the big day. They try in myriad ways to convince us that there are so many things we cannot do without any longer. Perhaps a cell phone upgrade, a brand new computer or, if you're somebody who literally has everything, a new sports car, will be the ticket to a memorable Christmas! If none of these are quite what you wanted, there is always Boxing Day (or Boxing Week now) to exchange what falls short of capturing your imagination for your heart's real desire. For still others, the big attraction of Christmas is often the fabulous unbridled feasting, snacking and drinking that "make the season so festive". Clusters of chocolates and hard candies sit in every room beckoning the passer-by to reduce the sweet burden of each bowl. Maybe the delicious smell of slowly cooked turkey with the best of stuffings and grandma's creamy mashed potatoes are your most sought after taste sensation of the holidays, along with the days of turkey-a la-king, turkey salad sandwiches and turkey soup that are incumbent on family members living under the same roof.

For still others the biggest attractions of the Christmas holidays are not found in the kitchen or under the tree. For them the biggest attraction is time off from work, quality time spent with family or friends or better yet a new love! "Mistletoe action" and fantasies about how romantic your sweetie would be to you and how you were going to make sure that your deepest inward desires would be met by him or her have long been the driving force for many during the Christmas season. Days off to frolic in the snow or misbehave at office and house parties around the end of the calendar can be much more enticing than the best of meals or gifts under the tree.

We all know, however, that real life and hoped-for life are two completely different things most of the time. For an increasing number of people, the Christmas period is one of deep loneliness, depression and despair. Families are broken or falling apart. Times are tough and often do not provide enough extras for folks to even contemplate luxuries like fine feasting or indulging oneself in some sinful little pleasures. We're burdened by unfulfilled hopes and dreams and a sense that these will NEVER, EVER be realized. So, what's the point of making a big deal about Christmas? It's just one of many religious holidays celebrated by certain people around the world who all essentially dream about the same things while collectively failing miserably to hit any of these visionary targets.

The answer to the point of Christmas is not to be found in any of the things that surround the special holiday. They're not found in the presents others have bought for us or in the parties of celebration or in the decorations or in the familiar Christmas music. The answer to the question of what we need for Christmas is simply found in the narrative account surrounding the birth of Jesus. The advent of Jesus Christ into human experience about 2000 years ago was unlike any other heralded birth of a celebrated teacher or leader. First of all, Jesus' birth had been foretold over 500 years before he arrived. The circumstances were very particular. There could be no mistaking it. He was not to be trumpeted in as a king but as a humble peasant. He was not to be born amongst the elite of Jewish or Roman society but instead would be easily entertained by shepherds and commoners. He was not to be born in an important city or commercial centre but in a little hick town up in the hills. A heavenly sign would be given to show God's chosen place and time. Strangers from other cultures would realize who this was before the establishment in power ever would! It's quite extraordinary that such a low-wrung person received such prophetic attention particularly in the ancient world where such things were reserved strictly for the kings and top officials in the court.

Only a small handful of people were expecting Christ's arrival but the accounts of their faithfulness are with us to this day. A man named Simeon had been told years before Jesus' arrival that he would not die before seeing the Saviour of Israel. When baby Jesus was brought to him for the ceremonial event of circumcision as the Jewish law required, Simeon at once realized that this was God's chosen one carried before him. The scripture records that Simeon said that he was ready to die now that he had beheld the Lord's Christ. Jesus' mother Mary had been told by an angel she would conceive and bare a son who would be the Saviour, not only of the Jews, but of all people! The angels who appeared to the shepherds tending their flocks in the fields at night repeatedly sang "Glory to God in the Highest and on earth peace towards men on whom His favour rests"! God's favour resting on you and me!? Come on! Who are you trying to kid? Try telling that to one of those poor guys beheaded in Iraq or killed by bombs around the world or to the family who lost their child in a house fire or the countless millions of abject poor in places around the globe from which the world's wealthy have turned their faces!

In a politically correct western world, a common response to the traditional Christmas story is simply to dismiss it as a parochial folk tale or myth that some people take way too seriously and try to force on everybody else. I would ask you to consider one important fact: Jesus never forced himself on anybody but his claims were bold. It was Jesus who told his listeners to "let your 'yes' be yes and your 'no' be no (in other words tell the truth all the time with no stretches or games). Jesus didn't bring "a kind of truth" or "truth for his time". Instead he said "I am THE truth and THE life and THE way. Nobody comes to the Father but through me". Nobody can mistake what he says here. He says to trust what he tells you because he is God! Hey, Jesus was a great teacher. He had great ideas that make living together better but believing he is God is taking things way too far!

So don't be so quick to dismiss the One who gave you the ultimate gift – a chance at life! Not only has God breathed into you and all your ancestors the breath of life but when things were at their worst He gave his most precious possession – what the Bible calls "His only Son whom He loves". Many of us are not entirely sure how this doctrine of the Trinity of God really works. Other belief systems ridicule this as nothing more than polytheism thinly veiled in monotheistic language. There is a profound reason why the doctrine of the Trinity is attacked so relentlessly – to misdirect people from the awesome truth that we have in Christmas. It is this: the very same Almighty God who spoke the universe into existence at a moment, loved you and I so much and our despair grieved His heart so profoundly that He gave Himself as a sacrifice to meet the terms of His own judgment for our rebellion! Yes, Jesus, Almighty God in human flesh, lowered Himself from the power and glory of heaven to be conceived as a helpless fetus, born as an equally helpless baby and subjected to all forms of temptations similar to what we have experienced throughout his childhood and early adult life.

The sweet story of baby Jesus born on the fluffy hay in some immaculate barn where the animals were practically serenading him is not the reality of who he is or why he came. God's whole purpose in sending Jesus was to give humanity a hope for everlasting life with God. We were and are powerless to do anything on our own to win God's favour. Our desire to "follow our own hearts" as so many tell us we need to do to be happy in today's world, has only alienated us from God and sealed our own fate by our own selfishness and self-promotion. Which of these slogans will you give in to this holiday season? "I'm worth it", "You can't please everybody so you might as well please yourself", "Have things your own way" or "Whoever has the most toys at the end, wins"?

The big deal about Christmas, as opposed to any other religious or non-denominational, non-gender specific, festive celebration held in the early winter of the year – or any other time for that matter – is simply this: God, more than anybody else, including each one of us, knows exactly what each of us needs for Christmas this year! Don't forget, it is He who has made us and not we ourselves. He sees more clearly than we ever can that we aren't just "down a bit", we are drowning! We are about to go under to never come up again! He offers us a solution – a life vest ready to buoy us to the surface. He has already made the gift and offered it to us. He offers us life-long satisfaction and joy. He offers the help of God in each of our lives! How could anybody say no to that? Unfortunately, the depth of our self-delusion and the gravity of our own problems has, like a drowning man, made us so focused on our own dire situation that we often can't see clearly enough that someone has come to save us from death's grip!

Despite the fact the water is filling up in our lungs and we can hardly get our mouth above the surface to gasp another breath, all we need to do is acknowledge this one who is there to help us. Give him your hand. Receive the one gift that will forever satisfy your heart and soul. Man doesn't live by the things he gets but by the positive things he gives to the lives of others. This is our biggest collective need this Christmas and always. Take time this Christmas to understand the greatness of the biggest present of all – learning what it means to truly live.

Geoff Bernardo

Chapter Thirteen

Christmas passed, we were back again to Pembroke and Geoff started his work again. We didn't get any good news from his office whether or not the permanent job would come for him while his contract ended at the end of February 2005. We were hopeful but he didn't want to just sit and wait, he started to look for new vacant positions elsewhere. He kept telling me about the offer from the people at work to apply for the position as Planner which was open for a while. He was a Planner years back when he was working in City of London, but he didn't do much more ever since he quitted from the job so he was not sure about this open position but most of his co-workers encouraged him to apply, that certainly gave him a big contribution to give it a try.

Geoff's contract was not extended nor the permanent job was available for him not because he was not qualified for the job but the budget was not yet available for that year so we went back home to Cavan. His manager really wanted him to stay, she was so comfortable to work with him but couldn't do much to keep him there. I didn't see any disappointment on his face, he had been ready for that, but I could feel his burden to start looking all over again and that means he needed to put a great number of time searching for the job on the internet. I remembered one early morning, probably the time was still 3 o'clock, I didn't see him on the bed so I went down just to check or call him to go to bed. He could spend hours and hours on the computer, he needed to take rest. Just as I suspected, he was sitting by his computer doing something.

"I am looking for the job, Honey, it might be too late if I should wait until late morning, I should act fast", he explained. I couldn't do anything else to get him back to bed, again he had my sympathy. I really needed to do something to help him out even though it would be just a little bit.

"How much do you think the proper price of my card if I want to sell it, Honey?" I asked him one morning when he came to see Phoebe who was playing in her playpen in our family room. I was sitting next to her, making more cards.

"Hmmm, let's see, since it's handmade and you spent hours to make one and it's your original design, I would say seven bucks is fine. Your cards are nice, too," he answered.

I told him about my idea to sell my cards on-line but I was not so sure about the rules and ethics to own a business here in Canada. Since he had such an experience, he explained to me more.

"I am going to take you to Peterborough if you plan to open a business and how it should be done, you need to register your business name, phone, etc. You need to provide them with some information and pay, but it's not much, probably fifty bucks", he added.

I was getting more and more interested so I started to make a website for my cards. I managed to create my personal website months back and I got so many feedbacks from the people who had seen it that it was nicely done so I would make another and this time for my business. Geoff had ever asked me to create one website for his own business but I couldn't start it without any information needed to be put there, he was still too busy to provide me with any. He had a big dream one day when he said he would activate his own business again, him as the President Director and me as the Vice President.

However, it was not easy to get the free time to do that, I had to prioritize Phoebe, do things in the house and yet the computer which had everything on it was always busy for Geoff to do his project. He needed both of his computer and laptop working together especially when he was downloading some files from the internet which could take days and nights. That was why I cherished the time when he was free and let me use it, I really utilized the time he gave to me. There were moments when he wanted me to sit together with him watching TV when Phoebe was already on bed, but I just kept sitting and working on my website even though he was trying to get my attention by saying there was a so and so program on TV or something like "Honey, it's about tsunami in Aceh, interesting, don't you want to see it?" or else he came to me and kissed my head asking, "What are you doing?" even though he knew that I was still working on my website.

He missed my company, I knew that, but I had to finish my project so I could think of more things to get my home business started. He opened the door to me anyway so he would understand it. I was so busy and excited, probably too excited to have it done that I didn't clean up the house as often as I did before. Our living room where I was doing my cards while looking after Phoebe who looked happy to play in her playpen was so messy with so many craft papers and tools on the floor but I still did cook and prepare our meals even though the time for us to have lunch and supper was getting later and later. We had to go back to our previous schedule, I whispered to myself, just little time to go then I was done.

Geoff seemed to have to face some bitter things in his life lately. He was so fanatic to sports of any kind and of course he stood for Canada but Canada didn't do much to win the games to make him pleased. Stanley Cup went to

US, World Cup went to US, Skating was not successful, Mike Weir didn't make a good result, Toronto Raptors were not as great as he hoped for, anything else? You can add the list probably.

As to the news, homosexual marriage was something which bothered him so much. He kept commenting about it showing his disappointment and anger to see such a thing would be allowed in Canada. "I don't hate gay people, but their action is something I totally disagree with. What God says sin is sin, no tolerance to that, we need to speak that up," he said. Sometimes I needed to make him calm by saying that nothing much we could do other than praying for the government that God will reveal the truth to them someday or probably God has a purpose to let it happen.

Garbage was another thing that he complained about. "I've never seen Peterborough as dirty as today. So much garbage I saw along the roads; papers, Tim Horton's cups, cans, straws, even baby's diaper, can you believe that? It looks so awful!" I knew he was upset but again, he never raised his voice when saying that. The same responses I got from him when we passed by Markham and Toronto. "Canada is a rich country but I don't understand why the government does not have the budget to pay some people to pick up the garbage and clean up the roads. Bet,

Vancouver has started cleaning up for the Olympic by now, I can't imagine if it hasn't yet."

He taught me many times how to select the garbage, which and which should go to which and which so I became an expert on that, something which I have never done before when I was in Indonesia, and I found it so fun to go to the transfer station putting the garbage away!

Chapter
Fourteen

"I was so sure that Pembroke will call me for an interview for that Planner post but it's been three weeks now, I haven't yet heard anything from them", Geoff said to me one day.

"Why don't you call them and ask, Honey? That's nothing wrong to do that and you will get the information right away", I suggested. I was again working on my cards, I became more and more skilled on that, I have never even thought I would love to do crafts.

"Well, I'll wait until tomorrow, if nothing happens then I will call. I'm expecting a call from this magazine guy, he said he would call me back but as I suspected, he never did so I'm going to call him again", he pulled the chair and started to dial.

Geoff's voice suddenly distracted my concentration when I was putting the papers on the card one by one. "There are so many people who get a job easily and yet they lack the responsibility for what they are doing. Here I am who commit to work well and do my best, why am I difficult to get one?" he sounded frustrated for the first time in my life I heard that. He must be disappointed with the responses of that guy with whom he just talked to. I just don't understand either why it was so difficult for him to get a job, someone who holds an MA Degree from one of the best universities in this country and most of all, someone who has commitment and passion in completing his tasks.

My heart ached for my husband's difficult times. I really wanted to make him successful in many things, but such a time seemed to not happen yet, probably someday.

His patience was again tested when finally he found out that the Planner job in Pembroke was given to somebody else. He felt upset not because he didn't get the job but his "friends" including some important people in Human Resources that he knew there, encouraged him to apply for the position and yet he was not called even for an interview at all. Even though he was upset, he kept saying that he was not worried he didn't get a job at all. It's just the matter of time. Another job that he was waiting to get the contract from them in Windsor, Essex, did not go to him either. He was one of the strong candidates they got and he was ready to move there for good even though he said that he didn't like the area. "It's so flat like a pancake", he gave his comment about it to me one day.

Call after call, interview after interview, nothing seemed to work for him until he got another chance when a company in Halton called him. He didn't look enthusiastic, answered the call plainly probably he didn't want to put too much hope this time. The date and time for the interview had been set up and he made himself ready for this interview.

As usual, he dressed up professionally, a nice shirt, pants and tie. When I saw him, I almost laughed because he put the tie too short to make him look like a clown, so I asked him to fix it. But then he came back again with the unchanged position of his tie and said, "Hi, my name is Geoff, it's great to meet you," offering his hand to shake with his funny voice like Donald Duck. He was acting. I laughed so hard, he was so funny and playful. That was another part of his characters, keeping his childhood traits. He loved to tickle me, he wouldn't stop until I tickled him back and I could be more aggressive than him in this area. He made me so shocked one night when he knew he couldn't stop me, so he did a trick. He stopped laughing, held his breath, lied down with eyes and mouth open with his tongue sticking out. He looked horrible that way and made me frightened thinking that he might have got heart attack. When I touched him, he said "boo!" and laughed hard. Another time, he hid behind the door one night when I just turned off the light ready for bed. He came out from his hiding place, slightly grabbed my shoulders from the back without saying anything. I was shocked! He just loved to tease me a lot!

He looked so handsome with that outfit even though he complained about his weight now that most of his pants were already too tight for him but no one would know that he wore the same pants over and over again. He was not really healthy at that time, it's been a week he got cold so I prayed for him the other night that he would get better for this interview.

Halton is close to where his sister and his parents live, so even though he doesn't like the city life, he was hopeful he could get a job there. "I really want to live closer to my parents now, Honey, I want to help and look after them if my sister dies," he said in a weak voice. I know he didn't like to say this but he had been prepared to see Karen dies because her condition didn't show any significant progress. This was another reason why we postponed our trip to see my family in Indonesia even though his dad allowed us to go but he didn't want to go. "I wouldn't enjoy my trip in Indonesia if we go now especially with my sister's health condition like today. I want to be around her when she dies," he said to me one night when we were still in Pembroke.

He did do the interview in Halton well, he was so happy for that and so hopeful that he was going to be selected from among other candidates to work there. "We need to put this house ready for sell now", he said, so he made some minor repairs to the house and painted the fences to make them look better and fresh.

His cold was not yet over, it even worsened. He got more headaches, coughed a lot and couldn't sleep at all. I became worried, I asked him to go to the hospital but as I suspected, he didn't want to. "I'll be fine, it's just a cold", his answer again didn't surprise me. When he was coughing, he always complained about the phlegm he felt in his chest that didn't want to come out. He kept forcing to get it out but failed. He also sneezed a lot, so hard and so many times. I knew he was allergic to dust but that time all seemed to come together at the same time. His body temperature was in normal range but I could feel that some parts of his body were cold and some were warm.

"Honey, can you imagine if this happens in your mom's house in Indonesia, it's a good thing that we are not there now," he said to me one night at the kitchen while drinking his cold water. His cold was not over yet. I several times asked him to drink warm water or at least room temperature when he was having cold, but he didn't want to. "Warm or room temperature water doesn't quench my thirst," he excused.

"When I was taking Phoebe upstairs, my breath was heavy," he said to me one evening from Phoebe's room when I was working on my website. I could hear it through the monitor we put at his computer room so we would know when Phoebe awakes or cries. I really wanted my website to get finished fast, whether or not I was too confident but I really wanted to get the income to help running the house. I didn't go up there right away, spent some more minutes with the computer and went to see them in Phoebe's room afterwards. Both him and Phoebe were laughing and playing, one of his favourite times when he was with Phoebe. He looked fine.

Geoff was not getting better the next day. He still couldn't sleep at all, he got more and more headaches, he felt stiff on the left side of his neck and jaw. He still tried to get the phlegm out from his chest, he did it really hard. He finally had the time to be able to sleep, that was on Sunday afternoon but he put a wet cloth on his forehead and let the radio run loudly. It was strange but I didn't comment. "Honey, please see the doctor", I asked him again but he was just quiet.

Sunday morning, we didn't go to the church because of his condition. We had to cancel our trip to see his parents and Karen too on Saturday, we planned to celebrate both Phoebe's and Karen's birthday together. It was going to be the first birthday party for Phoebe so we bought hats and paper trumpets for that but now it needed to get postponed. I put Vicks Vaporub on his back and rubbed it until red marks appeared. "In Indonesia it is said that the red marks indicate that you got so much wind inside your body," I told him.

He took a shower afterwards, he felt much better. I was happy but that didn't take long. After watching a movie on TV until around 1.30 a.m. we went to bed together but I noticed that he couldn't sleep again. He went to the bathroom, probably taking something, tried to sleep but still he couldn't. He got up and went down probably to the kitchen to take some drinks or to his computer room to work on something, I don't know because I fell asleep right away. Geoff used to be so hungry in the middle of the night so he would go down to the kitchen to drink a glass of milk or get some snacks but I am not sure what he did that night.

Monday morning, 7 o'clock, I got up and didn't find Geoff on the bed. He got to be working in his computer room or got up so early today, I talked to myself, so I came down to the kitchen to check. Phoebe was still sleeping, she usually got up at 8 o'clock or later then I would take her with me to our bedroom to spend some time with her playing. She loved playing with her daddy and mommy. She always pointed at the pictures that Geoff put there on the top of our bed's shelf. There are his picture alone, my picture alone, Karen's picture alone, the picture of Karen and him by the beach when they were small and our engagement picture. That morning she would not get such a nice time again.

I called Geoff, but no answer. While standing on the kitchen floor, I saw him in his computer room but he was lying down on the floor there. I had no bad thought at all as to what has happened, I thought he finally could sleep even though he had to sleep on the floor.

"Why are you sleeping here, Honey?" I asked while approaching him. I saw his face, his eyes were open, he lifted up his right hand trying to reach me while saying something but it was so unclear to me. I thought he was being playful again but minutes later, I then realized something bad had happened to him. I couldn't hold my emotion for not screaming. I got shocked! Totally shocked! I called him over and over again, but no good reaction. My chest was so hurt for screaming that loud, I didn't care! I screamed and I cried! I got so crazy! I finally could grab what he was saying. He asked me to help him sit up. I did, but I was so weak and he was so heavy that he fell again. I screamed again, calling his name, I was so panic, so scared, so frightened, so terrified. I finally could help him sit up but not in a perfect position. I couldn't do any better. He was totally disabled! He couldn't move his body at all! I ran to the telephone to call 911 but it was connected to the computer. I didn't want to waste time, I ran out to my neighbour, Steve and Jenny, with bare feet and my pajamas. I knocked their door so hard, I shouted and shouted loudly calling them, when finally Jenny came out from her bedroom with eyes still looked sleepy, I grabbed her arms.

"Jenny, where is Steve? Where is he? I need him to help Geoff, he is dying, he is dying!" I cried and screamed which made her panic as well. I couldn't stop crying and screaming, I couldn't talk to 911 operator clearly when she asked what I needed, the police or the ambulance, finally with all power I could collect, I managed to tell her.

I thought Geoff was already gone when I ran back from Jenny's house. He was still alive. I stroke his head, his face, his cheeks. I was so scared he would die. "Honey, please don't leave me, please...!" I cried, hugging him but he didn't give any reaction to me. Within ten minutes, the 911 guys came and checked him. He could answer all their questions correctly, his memories were still good. He was rushed to the hospital, they let me go with him in that big ambulance. I was so confused, I couldn't tell how my feelings were at that time.

He was then put in the emergency room, some other patients were there but all of them were older people. The doctor and nurses checked him. He still could communicate with me with his weak voice. As I suspected, he got stroke, but how bad, I had no idea until the result of his brain scanning came.

I had a talk with the doctor who told me that Geoff got a severe stroke. It was bad, really bad. He'd been so healthy during his life, he never smoked, he never drank, he was always so active and fit, he had never been hospitalized for a single time, so now he got stroke. It's not fair. I would never know why he got it, was he so stressful for not being able to get a job and think of so many things on his mind?

I cried again, one nurse came and hugged me, offered me to meet with a social worker there just to have a chat and get accompanied. I forced myself to realize that it was real, really real. My husband would be disabled and I had to be ready with that. I wanted to call his parents but I forgot their number, you will not believe this but I got the correct number from Geoff!

I got his mom on the phone, it was so hard to tell her but I managed. Being a soft-spoken lady, she didn't scream but I know she was shocked. Their only daughter was really sick and now their only son got stroke!

I needed someone to be with me. I called Pastor Rick, but he was away somewhere. I called my neighbour, Cathy, she was coming. My father-in-law and Pastor Peter called me while I was talking to the doctor who asked me to tell him what had happened with Geoff, what he had done, what he had taken, what he complained about, everything I could remember. I couldn't hold my tears again when Geoff's parents and Pastor Peter came. Geoff was still able to talk to them but not really much.

The next day, he was moved to another room where the nurses are available 24 hours. His condition didn't show any better, he was getting drowsier and drowsier, but he still remembered people and tried to communicate with them. More and more people from our church heard about Geoff and they visited him and prayed for him at the hospital. He even had a chance to ask me one day about Phoebe and expressed his concerns when I told him that Phoebe was fine and with Jenny now. He knew Jenny has dogs and cat so he was concerned that Phoebe might get allergic to them just like he was. I asked him for not getting worried about that.

He lifted up his left hand to get something, I was glad that finally he could move his left hand. His brain was damaged that he didn't recognize the side of what is called "left" but then he realized it.

"Are you going to do something, Honey?" I asked him when his hand was swaying.

"I want to touch your hair."

I took his hand and put it on my head. He started to stroke.

"What's this?" he asked.

"That's my hair, why?"

"How come it's so rough?"

If he weren't sick that way, I would laugh getting such an answer from him because I knew how much he loved my hair which he said so silky and soft but I knew he was serious so he must feel that my hair was so rough to his hand, probably just like a broom. My heart ached. I really wanted to be with him and talk to him for longer time but the room was so packed with the patients and equipments so no privacy at all not to mention the limited time for visiting and Geoff's weak condition to talk, so I decided to go home. I said goodbye.

"I'll be back again, Honey. I love you. Have a good rest!"

"I love you. Have fun with Phoebe!"

My heart cried.

Chapter Fifteen

Geoff's condition was getting worse, he got drowsier and drowsier and the doctor said it was not good. He was moved to another higher ICCU room and they put his brain and his lungs "rest" for the time being and the machine was taking over the functions. The doctor said it was meant to get his condition better but the result of his MRI showed that the damage in the tissues of his brain already happened and it swelled more, nothing they could do to make it better.

At the third day he was there, he couldn't communicate at all, his eyes were just closed, no reaction to touches, nothing at all. I cried again, again and again. I was still hopeful that he was going to be better the next day, I asked God to give miracles to him, to me, to his parents, to Karen, to Phoebe, until that night, when I was finished talking over the phone to his dad who just arrived back in his house in Mississauga updating me with Geoff's latest condition, I listened to the message I got from his doctor at the hospital that Geoff's condition worsened and he was sorry to tell me that Geoff couldn't live any longer soon! I cried out loud! I was so broken-hearted. I wanted to die. I felt like half of my body was gone. I felt like I didn't stand on the earth anymore. I felt like flying to an uncertain place. I phoned his dad and told him about the phone message I just got from the hospital while crying and sobbing. He asked me to give the phone to Sue, one of Geoff's cousins, who stayed to accompany me, then he asked her to call the hospital to find out the details. She also called Pastor Rick to help take me to the hospital. I was so sad, really sad. Something which scared me a lot that Geoff was going to die before me now happened. I couldn't believe it. He was gone so fast, so so fast. Few minutes after I got that sad news, I heard Phoebe crying. Oh, Phoebe, oh, Phoebe, she knew that her loving daddy was going to say goodbye soon yet she didn't get any last kiss from him!

With Pastor Rick and his wife, Wendy, at Geoff's room, I sat down by his bedside stroking his head, hand and face. "Honey, I really want you to come back to me but you belong to The Lord, He wants you to come back to Him now, He has the authority. I love you so very much! I will never ever forget you in my life. I will tell Phoebe how amazing you have been. See you in heaven!" I whispered in his ear.

My tears rolled, hugged and kissed him for the last time. Oh, it was so sad. It was so hurt to see my mom crying when my dad passed away many years back, and now right before my eyes I had to see my husband gone too.

Me, my father-in-law, Pastor Rick, Pastor Peter, four of us in the hospital meeting room, talking about our plan where and when was going to be the best time for Geoff's funeral. He was already gone by the time we got there, Wednesday, April 27, 2005 at 11 p.m. and we already prayed to deliver him to the Lord, but we needed to get the official statement from the doctor which we got the next day pronouncing his death on Thursday, April 28, 2005 at 8.15 a.m. I couldn't believe I had the strength to face these all even I could still remember that Geoff wanted to donate his organs. He encouraged me to do the same, he signed up my health card for his support.

No tears in my eyes, no sobs, no emotions, when I signed all the papers to let his organs taken. My father-in-law was with me when I was signing all documents. It was a very horrible thing to do but I just felt numb, totally numb, I was just like a robot doing what I was asked to do. My father-in-law asked me if I wanted to spend more time with Geoff in his room, I said no. I just couldn't stand to realize that it was only his body, his soul is with Jesus now and I cannot see and talk to him anymore.

On our way passing his room, the curtains which closed the room from public's eyes were open a bit, my eyes once again saw his body on the bed, so handsome, so peaceful, so calm. When he was still able to talk couple of days before, I had a chance to ask him whether he felt any pain anywhere in his body, he said no, I was happy to hear that. I also had a chance to tell him that he got an interview call for a job he applied at the government company he was really interested in, they even called twice, that might be an exciting news for him even though he might have known he couldn't make it. He's gone without any pain he had to fight with. He's gone just a week after Phoebe's first birthday. He's gone peacefully, as peaceful as his favourite picture with his canoe that he hung on the wall at our dining room at home.

Tuesday, May 3, 2005, is Geoff's funeral day. My mom, my sister Tin who had birthday at that time and my sister Oline who came to our wedding to be my bridesmaid, managed to come to Canada for the funeral. It was so amazing to hear how fast they got the visa to come to Canada, only within one hour! They put their application on Friday morning, just few minutes before the embassy closed, they got it! They all looked so tired, like having no sleep for a week! We had a chance to see Geoff's body for the last time in his cascade and I let my wedding ring stay in his finger before the cascade closed. That ring belonged to him, his earthly body, that once he married a girl in the earth, and she was me.

The funeral took place in Glen Oaks Memorial Gardens. A very nice cemetery, green huge lawn, quiet, all we could hear was just the songs of the birds. It was a very simple and nice ceremony, only the families and Geoff's best friends who were part of the pall bearers, came. The air was cold, the sky was dark and raining, looked gloomy, Geoff's body was buried in his favourite type of weather.

"One of the nicest things Geoff told me on one of his letters was how thankful he was to me for giving birth to you to be his wife," my mom said to me after the funeral. "I was so happy to get his words, I will always remember that, nobody has even ever had a thought to say that to me," she continued.

I hugged her. She missed Geoff so much, so did my entire family in Indonesia. They had planned to hold a big celebration for us should we come to visit them, to get both him and Phoebe introduced to the rest of the family.

The service at Chartwell Baptist Church was done so nicely. Both of our pastors at the wedding, Pastor Peter and Pastor Polin, and our pastor from Ferndale church in Peterborough, Pastor Rick, led the ceremony. Hundreds of people came even Karen. She sat on the wheel chair at the back pew, I was happy she could come even though her condition was so weak. I needed to meet her and give her something. Something that Geoff was preparing at the day he fell in his computer room. I just needed to have it ready.

The service was opened with the hymn: "It Is Well With My Soul" which me and Geoff liked so much. My heart broke, really broke. We used to listen to this hymn in the car, over and over again yet I sang this song for my husband's funeral service. Many people cried for us and they felt more empathy to my parents-in-law when at the same time they were still having a burden for their loving daughter, Karen, Geoff's sister, who was really ill. These people, including me myself were all amazed with their strong faith. I was more amazed to see them that during these sad times, they were still strong to arrange everything for the funeral and memorial service.

I don't know how many people I met, talked and hugged after the service, it was like having visitors at the wedding. Many of our church friends from Peterborough and Pembroke came while the distance is far enough to get to Mississauga where the ceremony was held. Pastor Alan from our church in Pembroke was there as well. He mentioned to me he would always remember the early morning when I called him to pray for Geoff who was sick. He had a chance to pray for Geoff who came to the altar at the last Sunday we attended his church.

Seeing them all made me more emotional as if I was seeing Geoff standing among them. Geoff's friends from all over the places even from United States, came. I had a chance to get to know some of them whom Geoff told me a lot yet I've never met. Scott cried when I told him that a week before Geoff died, he was looking forward to go fishing with him but he was still away in Cuba with his wife, Kelly.

Together with Geoff's parents, uncle, aunt and cousins, we had supper at his parents' house after the service at the church. Karen was too sick to join so she stayed on bed upstairs. While having supper, Geoff's dad read the letter prepared by my sister, Kindeng, representing the entire families in Indonesia, how much they missed Geoff even though they just saw him only through pictures. Kindeng is my only sister who never met with Geoff face to face. Actually my other sister, Tin, never met with him either, it was just his body she saw. She will never forget Geoff saying on the phone to her how much he liked her homemade cake that my mom and Oline brought when they came for our wedding.

I was so tired, I really needed some good rest but I knew I couldn't. I don't know how I should face my days without Geoff anymore. I just don't know. Everything would be so much different without him. No more fishing stories. No more fun experiences. No more excited voice at the door calling me and Phoebe. No more plans to go canoeing or seeing salmon in Port Hope. No more Geoff who made any day special.

Oh, Canada! I see your beauty in my husband's life and now he is gone, will I still see it in you? In the silence of Cavan, my mind rolled back to each year I have passed. 2002, I came here for our marital course. 2003, we got married. 2004, we got a baby. 2005, my husband died. 2006, 2007, 2008 ... what then, please Lord?

He is gone without having the chance to get a new job, to get his fishing book published, to get his mapping project finished, to get our house sold, to get me treated in the spa or salon as one of his Christmas gifts, to visit my families in Indonesia, to buy a digital camera for his dad as a Christmas gift, to take me ice-fishing, to take me and Phoebe boating and canoeing, to take me and Phoebe to Banff, to spend vacation in a log house, to help me get my business name registered, to unpack some of our wedding gifts, to buy our dining set as our wedding gift from his parents, even to finish his final will.

He is gone. My dearest loving and caring husband is gone. It took seven years for me to get him to be mine but only for two years he was mine. What a precious nine years I had with him!

Chapter Sixteen

Karen was on the bed when I met with her at her room. She cried when she knew I was bringing something that Geoff made for her as a birthday gift. She asked for my permission for not opening it right away, I knew she needed time for that. I found the article that Geoff made about his past life with her on his office desk so I knew he was preparing this for her at the time I found him on the floor of his computer room. He kept asking me any gift idea for her birthday but then he seemed to find what he was going to do and he didn't tell me what. He just asked me to see and wait. My job was to make a birthday card ready for her.

When I found that article, some pictures of them both and an album, I didn't know what I was going to do with them. I was scared that Karen would be sadder if she got it but I really wanted her to know how much Geoff loved her. With tears in eyes, I managed to put things altogether in the album and give it to her. I didn't know what her reaction would be when opening it, seeing the pictures and reading the article, something that Geoff prepared at his last breath, she deserved it and I was happy to be able to do it for both of them. I was happy to be able to talk to Karen over the phone for an hour and listened to her happy voice after I gave Geoff's gift to her.

I had to think more seriously about my and Phoebe's future now. Being a single parent who has no job and never had any job in a foreign country with a little baby, people might think I'm crazy to still want to live here in Canada. I am not, I am not crazy, I am doing it for strong reasons.

Months and months before Geoff died, he mentioned to me how much he wanted Phoebe to get raised and educated in Canada. He also gave the names of the people who might be the best people, Christian couples, for Phoebe's custodians if something happens to both of us. At the other hand, his parents, Phoebe's grandparents, will still be able to help financially and spiritually.

Phoebe is a Canadian, Indonesia doesn't recognize two nationalities, so better if Phoebe lives in Canada as a Canadian than in Indonesia as a foreigner even though it is her mother's home country. I know the decision is in my hands now and it is tough, but I won't make any decision without any reasons so Lord willing, we are going to live in Canada, at least, we try.

There are so many things I have to work on after Geoff died. Paying the bills, closing his active accounts, notifying people about his death, many more to list. I am willing to get his book published as well but I know it is not going to be easy and fast as I am not the expert on the fishing things but his dad will help. He really helps me a lot in so many things especially in settling his will, I had no idea how it should work. He back and forth traveled to Cavan and we back and forth traveled to Peterborough to have meetings with the lawyers and bank. My mom who still stayed with me in Canada for a while at that time was a great help to look after Phoebe when I was away. We planned to go to Indonesia together.

Friday, June 10, I called my father-in-law in his office about some tasks I have done, he was not there so I put a message on his phone. I had no idea how he managed to finish his work at the office without Karen's assistance, that must be so tiring for him to do it all alone. Just few minutes after I hung up, I got his call. Cheerfully I greeted him and told him that I just gave him a message but he said he was not at the office.

"The reason I'm calling you, Vita, is to tell you that Karen passed away this morning at around 4 o'clock!" he said calmly.

I couldn't believe what I had heard! We had been all prepared to know the possibility that Karen would die but still it was a shock when I heard it. I am glad God gives me tears so I can cry. "But she asked you for not postponing or canceling your trip to Indonesia if she dies and we need to respect that," he added. He knew what I was going to say. I begged him to let me stay for her funeral, he firmly said no.

Not so many experiences I had with Karen but I have many things to tell about her characters and my relationship with her and how special she was to her brother, Geoff. Her body was going to be buried in the same cemetery, side by side with Geoff. She is gone just six weeks after Geoff died. Someday I'll be with them too.

Monday, June 13, my parents-in-law took us to the airport. The tears never wanted to go away from me yet. After so many things happened in my life recently, now I had to leave my parents-in-law as we were going to Indonesia. The body of their daughter was still in the funeral home when they were taking us to the airport and now they had to see me and Phoebe go far. I would be in the sky in my anniversary, June 14, first anniversary without my loving husband but it doesn't have any meaning now. There will be no anniversary for me anymore without him around.

Chapter Seventeen

Phoebe was sound asleep, I could hear the rhythm of her breath, softly. I stopped patting her, I ended my song with a humming rhythm while putting the blanket to cover half of her body. With the temperature of 24 degrees Celcius circled by the air conditioning, the room was cold enough for me but that was the temperature suggested by Phoebe's doctor to make her body temperature down. She had been sick for quite a while now, had to get hospitalized twice within just a week apart. She lost much of her weight so fast. That really scared me. The doctors found the virus in her digestive system and said that her body was adjusting to the new environment, new weather, new climate, her immune system was not yet ready for those things. They suggested me to go back to Canada once she got better.

I looked around the room, it was my room before I went to Canada to marry Geoff. It was the room where Geoff stayed for about two weeks on his first visit to meet with me and my family in Indonesia. It was also the room which was filled by his roses on the day he proposed to me. I saw our pictures on the wall, his on the left side, mine on the right side and Phoebe's in the middle, sitting on her highchair that his mom gave as her Christmas gift. Geoff took that picture at his lunch time in our apartment in Pembroke. Phoebe loves to see pictures, Geoff always spent his time to hold her walking around our family room pointing at the pictures. "This is Mommy, this is Daddy and this is Phoebe!" he said repeatedly and Phoebe keeps it in her memories. Whenever she sees Geoff's picture, she will shout, "Daddy ... Daddy!"

My family helped me a lot prepare the room for us. They tried to make it as comfortable as possible. My mom doesn't have a lot of money to have a spectacular room makeover just like I saw on TV, but it was clean and tidy enough. No bed in the room, just two mattresses on the floor to avoid a big fall for Phoebe in case she rolled over. Knowing that Phoebe several times got mosquito bites, my mom rushed to go to the market to buy the net fabric, built it by tying each of the four corners of the fabric with the string needled on the wall. It was so simple but helped us for not getting the mosquito bites. This made me remember Geoff saying, "We have to buy the net fabric for Phoebe if we are in Indonesia, the mosquitoes will bite her otherwise." He seemed to have known what was going to happen.

Just two days to go, we were going to go back to Canada. It was not going to be an easy travel especially with a little child in your arms, that was really not easy but I didn't want to postpone it anymore, the faster the better. I was missing our house in Cavan, far away from the city life, so quiet, so calm, so beautiful and I was not worried that it was broken being empty for four months because my parents-in-law and our neighbours, Steve and Jenny, were looking after it. They are kind-hearted people, I don't know what I should do without their kindness.

Our flight took off at 7 o'clock in the morning, that means we had to be at the airport at least by five o'clock. Phoebe was still in her pajamas when I took her from the bed, she got up wondering what has happened especially when she saw everyone was in tears when we said goodbye. She doesn't like to see tears. Several times she hit my face when she saw me crying, she just doesn't understand. But there was the time when she touched my tears, took it and looked at it carefully. That made my cry louder. She didn't understand that soon we were leaving Jakarta, leaving her grandma, uncles, aunties, cousins, leaving all people who gave her so much attention.

Even though I was already at the airport by four o'clock in the morning, still it took so long to get everything done. I was kissing my mom goodbye when the announcement came calling all passengers of Cathay Pacific going to

Hong Kong to get ready. Phoebe didn't want to be put in her stroller that John and Leanne gave to me, so I had to hold her in my arms while holding a heavy bag in left arm and another heavy bag in right arm plus another bag of her toys. I was shocked to read the information on the computer that my plane was already boarding, I ran and ran, I was scared I would stumble and fall for being so weak for not having a single sleep at all busily packing with my mom and sisters who helped me at the last night I was with them.

We got to the plane on time, I was so tired but felt relieved. I got a comfortable seat, the space in front of me was wide enough to put my things down there after the plane taking off. Phoebe was already on my lap, she seemed fine but that didn't take long, she wanted to go down. One stewardess said it was fine to let Phoebe walk for a while, the plane was delayed for fifteen minutes. But she was wrong. Within only two minutes and Phoebe was already free from my arms, the captain announced that we were going to take off anytime.

I took Phoebe back to my lap but, you could guess, she didn't want to. She started to scream and cry, she hit, she scratched, she bit, she pulled my hair, any behaviour that was just new to me coming from her. I failed to make her calm, she just cried out loud even until the plane was already stable in the sky. I didn't care what the other passengers thought and said, they might complain but I couldn't do anything. It was a good thing that we didn't sit at the business class seats! Phoebe is just a little child who might be frustrated because she was awakened so early in the morning, still so tired for getting awake for long hours the night before, she was so interested in the plane and wanted to explore more and yet her mommy just took her freedom away! So I didn't care, but I did apologize though to the young Chinese students who sat beside me if Phoebe was a problem for them. I thought the best respond I would get from them was just their bitter smile but it was not! One of them with his pleasant face smilingly said, "That's okay, she is just a baby". Oh, I was glad.

Being so tired from crying and screaming, Phoebe fell asleep with her sobs. I didn't know what I was going to do with her if she kept crying like that all the way to Toronto which took for about twenty seven hours! I even had a thought to just fly back to Jakarta right away. What a crazy idea! In fact, Phoebe became sweet, the weather for our flight from Singapore to Hong Kong was so nice that I could take Phoebe to walk along the isles. Many girls who were at the plane loved to see her, touched her, talked to her, even though she was a big problem for me an hour ago. I didn't have any problem at all on our trip from Hong Kong to Toronto which took for about seventeen hours. The seat beside me was empty, so I got more rooms for

Phoebe. She became sweeter, the plane crews loved to see her, I even got some helps from some passengers who sat beside me to look after her whenever I was going to the lavatory.

Friday, September 30 at around 10 p.m., our flight landed in Pearson Airport, Toronto. That reminded me again of my last flight on April 2003 to meet with Geoff for our wedding, the same view of the city looked from the sky, the same music that I heard at the plane but not the same excitement when the plane was about to land. Oh, how much I wished that he was waiting for us now at the airport to pick us up but I knew that was not going to happen.

At the immigration desk, it was a smooth process even though Phoebe started to get bored and wanted her milk but she got entertained by two big police dogs which were around the area that night. No problem at all with Phoebe who is a Canadian and me holding a Permanent Resident card for this immigration thing. With a great help from some porters at the airport who carried my four big-heavy suitcases, I didn't feel any burden at all but one of our suitcases had to go to the inspection desk. Two of Phoebe's milk which I bought from Jakarta were taken and checked whether they contained the ingredients which are forbidden to consume in Canada. They were good to go.

It took time to look for the face of my father-in-law at the airport. I was just thinking he was alone to pick us up there because my mother-in-law was having leg problem after falling from the stairs at their cottage. Even though it was already midnight, the airport was still so packed with people, those who were flying, arriving and picking up. I was looking around when my eyes caught two faces which I recognize so well. Ruth and Sue! Two of Geoff's cousins. Then I saw their parents, Aunt Marianne and Uncle Ed. Suddenly I saw a balloon with small fishes decorating it which was given to Phoebe. Oh, that was my mother-in-law! Her eyes were in tears when she greeted us. Finally, I saw my father-in-law, waiting sympathetically with his calm smile giving a warm kiss and long hug to me. I cried, I really cried to hug each of them one by one. I got a very nice bouquet from Sue, saying, "Welcome home and Happy Birthday, Vita!"

My birthday, yes, my first birthday without Geoff, was celebrated with my family in Jakarta. "Let's plan to visit your family on September, Honey, that will give us a chance to celebrate your birthday together with them too," Geoff's voice ringing in my ears. He didn't make it. He didn't even have the chance to celebrate his birthday, Mother's Day, Father's Day, our anniversary. Some other special days will come, special days without my beloved husband.

We stayed for one night in my parents-in-law's house before we head off to Cavan where our house is. It takes for about 1.5 hours to get there, sounds so long, but I always enjoy the trip especially on October, entering the Fall season, Geoff's favourite season, when the colour of the trees starts to change beautifully.

Our house still looked the same but the front yard has a little bit changed with some flowers that my parents-in-law put so now there are not just the green plants which sometimes got brown and dry. The grass looked just recently cut, so fresh and tidy, my neighbours helped me on that. There is one small tree which was bought by Geoff last Christmas, it's still there with more leaves on it. He ever said to me one day that we needed to bring that tree if we were going to move somewhere. That tree was special to him that he named it as "Phoebe's tree". Looking at the front door, how much I wanted to see him standing there welcoming us, one thing that I believe someday he will do it. He now lives in a very beautiful home, the most beautiful home which will never be designed and built in the world. A home which is prepared by the Lord Jesus, a home which doesn't have any hurt, pain, sadness, disappointment, anger, uncertainty and most of all ... death! Nothing but joy!

Seeing the house again, my emotions started to pile, I knew I would cry. I didn't really want to get out of the car right away, I was enjoying the memories to see the house outside, its big lawn where Geoff regularly mowed on

Summers using his own mower or borrowing Steve's riding mower if he was in a rush or feeling tired, raked the leaves before Winter comes, cleaned up the windows which sometimes made me worried that he would fall from the ladder he used which didn't look sturdy to me, and just few days before he got stroke, he had a chance to repaint the porch fence. On the wooden floor of the porch, I still could see the bird eggs he broke when he took the nest out of our mail box. He didn't know there were some eggs on the nest, he felt bad afterwards. He had a very sensitive and tender feeling about life. When we were in Bali, he couldn't eat well after seeing a mother holding a baby, who was probably not her baby, begging by the window of our cab. A very common thing happened in most of the cities in Indonesia but not in Canada.

Entering the house, I didn't get the unique smell of our house which we got for so long. This time it was the smell of the fresh paint. I was stunned to see the changes inside. My kitchen looked so new and fresh with a pretty lay out made by my mother-in-law who is, just like Karen said to me, genius in taking care of and decorating the house. All the bathrooms were newly painted, the toilet and the faucets are all new. They did this all for me and Phoebe without taking off the memories the house brings. I felt so full in my chest, I couldn't hold my tears anymore, I cried in my in-law's embrace. I cannot describe how thankful I am to them but I know that they are used by God to help me. I don't know what my future brings in this country but what I know is that God never leaves me. I lost my husband but the Lord sends so many people to care for us, to help us and to love us. My neighbours and the people in the church, He sends them to help us and most of all, my parents-in-law who are still grieving for losing all of their children.

I recalled one day when Geoff asked me if I want to be his parents' daughter. I was surprised to get this question, I found it strange why he asked me that, so I thought he was saying this to realize that Karen was going to die sooner or later. I felt flattered, I don't have any quality as Karen had so I answered humbly, "But I'm not Karen." There is no way that somebody else could take the place of Karen in their heart, but now I understand why Geoff asked me that. His parents have done so many things to help me just like they did to him and to Karen. I looked at my finger, I'm still wearing his ring, I don't want to take it off. He was so special to me. It will always remind me that once I married an angel in this earth.

Geoff's characters have impacted many souls. He loved the Lord, he loved the people, he always tried hard to give his best. Just like one of his friends said:

Courtesy of: Stephen Vass Photography

Geoffrey John Bernardo
(1961 – 2005)

"Rejoice in the Lord always. I will say it again: Rejoice!"
(Philippians 4:4)

Printed in the United States
45954LVS00001B/113

9 780977 492848